BLAZER**MANIA**

BLAZERMANIA

THIS IS OUR STORY

WRITTEN BY **WAYNE THOMPSON**   FOREWORD BY **BILL WALTON**

INSIGHT ◉ EDITIONS

San Rafael, California

All photos courtesy of the Portland Trail Blazers Image Archives, unless otherwise noted below:

Brian Bahr/Getty Images: 170; Bill Baptist/Getty Images: 132; Doug Beghtel/ The Oregonian: 168; Andrew D. Bernstein/Getty Images: 138–139, 142–143; Thomas Boyd/The Oregonian: 245; Cameron Browne/Getty Images: 229; Nathaniel S. Butler/Getty Images: 201; Chris Covatta/Getty Images: 170; Joel Davis/The Oregonian: 152, 157, 167, 179, 180, 186; Steve Dipaola/The Oregonian: 137, 172–173, 174–175, 176; Steve Dykes: 104–105; Todd Eckelman/ NBA Photos/Trail Blazers Inc.: 168; Bruce Ely/The Oregonian: 164–165, 180, 187, 188–189, 190, 192, 194, 195, 198, 199, 202–203, 204, 206–207, 208, 209, 210–211, 212, 213, 214–215, 218, 219, 222, 223, 224, 226–227, 228, 230–231, 232, 233, 234–235, 236, 237, 238–239, 240, 241, 249, 259, 262–263, 264; Sam Forencich/Getty Images: 161, 176, 180, 181, 183, 184–185, 186, 196–197, 242– 243; Jesse D. Garrabrant/Getty Images: 205; Otto Greule Jr./Getty Images: 241, 244; Andy Hayt/Getty Images: 182, 258; Roger Jensen/The Oregonian: 257; Fred Joe/The Oregonian: 178; Mike Lloyd/The Oregonian: 128–129, 140, 144, 145, 147, 148, 150–151, 153, 158–159, 261; Donald Miralle/Getty Images: 180; Joe Murphy/Getty Images: 216–217, 220–221; Steve Nehl/The Oregonian: 131, 132, 140; Thomas Oliver/Getty Images: 225; The Oregonian: 146; Mike Powell/ Getty Images: 130; Angela Pancrazio/The Oregonian: 171; Jennifer Pottheiser/ Getty Images: 191; Alan Spearman/The Oregonian: 177; Jim Taylor/The Portland Trail Blazers: 200, 204; Tom Treick/The Oregonian: 133, 149, 154; Brent Wojahn/The Oregonian: 162, 169.

Library of Congress Cataloging-in-Publication Data available.

ISBN: 978-1-60887-012-7

ROOTS of PEACE   REPLANTED PAPER

Insight Editions, in association with Roots of Peace, will plant two trees for each tree used in the manufacturing of this book. Roots of Peace is an internationally renowned humanitarian organization dedicated to eradicating land mines worldwide and converting war-torn lands into productive farms and wildlife habitats. Together, we will plant two million fruit and nut trees in Afghanistan and provide farmers there with the skills and support necessary for sustainable land use.

Manufactured in China by Insight Editions

10 9 8 7 6 5 4 3 2 1

INSIGHT EDITIONS
10 Paul Drive
San Rafael, CA 94903
www.insighteditions.com

CONTENTS

FOREWORD
BY BILL WALTON

MOSES CAME RIDING UP ON A QUASAR TO DELIVER
THE GREATEST STORY EVER TOLD . . .

—DR. BOB WEIR, PHILOSOPHER, POET LAUREATE, AND INTERGALACTIC EXPLORER

LIGHT A CANDLE—LET THE CELBRATION BEGIN

When you've been touched by something really special in your life, things are never quite the same again. You generally spend the rest of the time chasing down that magic, on the chance that it just might come round your way one more time.

So it began. The birth of a great nation. February 6, 1970. When Harry Glickman had the vision of grandeur that was to become his life—and ultimately ours.

Lewis and Clark came to Oregon more than 200 years ago on their journey to the Promised Land. When they finally arrived on the shores of the Pacific, they couldn't wait to get back home to let everybody know what treasures they had found.

One would almost think that we're seeing double. Harry Glickman—Lewis and Clark. Centuries apart, yet strikingly similar voyages of discovery and enlightenment that have become over time the two greatest legacies in the bountiful history of our wondrous land here in the Pacific Northwest.

We just celebrated for the fortieth time the brilliance of Harry's dream. And what a wild ride it's been.

From the grace and beauty of Geoff Petrie's first feathery jump shot all the way to Brandon Roy's classy, dignified, yet passionate dynamism, Blazer fans throughout the galaxies have seen it all.

Success in life can be measured in many ways. The Blazers have captured the eyes of the world across all the prisms of the spectrum.

With only three business owners in these 40 years, the organization has been sustained with the stability and consistent guidance that ultimate luminosity requires. As a fan, who could ask for more than what we all got from Herman Sarkowsky, Larry Weinberg, and now Paul Allen, supreme field commanders who were built to last and who always did whatever it took to get the job done, sacrificing nothing along the golden road to unlimited devotion.

From the lifelong commitment of Harry Glickman to Larry Miller's stewardship today, we are reminded what Magellan, Captain Cook, and Charles Darwin meant for our evolutionary and manifest destiny.

From Hall of Fame coaches Lenny Wilkens and Jack Ramsay all along the watchtower to Nate McMillan gleaming in the golden light of day, we have all learned life's greatest lessons from our master teachers. They made all of us better than we could possibly have become on our own. They turned the light on and illuminated the path to glory.

From a front office staff in the early days that numbered barely more than a handful to the 300-plus that it now takes to launch the greatest show on Earth—where every want and need is literally catered to.

A litany of the sport's greatest players have blessed this organization with their heart, spirit, and soul, baring their blood, sweat, and tears for all to witness. Sidney Wicks, Maurice Lucas—the greatest of them all—Lionel Hollins, Bob Gross, and the rest of the championship squad from the 1970s. Clyde Drexler, Buck Williams, Terry Porter, and Jerome Kersey. Arvydas Sabonis. And now the incandescent Brandon Roy.

But this is a team game, contributed to magnanimously for generations by legions of lucky, happy, selfless true believers on the spirit road. Really, it's been the game of life played magnificently on the grandest of stages for 40 years now. Who would ever have thought? Portland? Oregon? Lewis and Clark? Harry Glickman? May the fire on the mountain burn forever.

The city of Portland, the state of Oregon, the world, all have changed dramatically in the decades since Harry Glickman's and Lewis and Clark's dreams came to fruition.

Western civilization—Memorial Coliseum, a.k.a. the Glass Palace—the early practice sites that sometimes left you scratching your head and casting wary, sideways glances. To the temple that is today's Rose Garden—yes, dreams do come true. Could things really be any better?

Along the roller coaster ride that has taken us down so many roads, two things have remained constant as our shining star, moral compass, and beacon of hope.

First, Bill Schonely. The grandest and most important Blazer of us all. Bill Schonely. The Bridge. The Rock. The Foundation. The Conduit. The man who makes it possible for all of us to believe. He is the force of nature that makes us all better than we really are. The man who gives us purpose, direction, and a reason to believe—without which we have nothing.

Second, the Blazer fans—the people who have given us the greatest life that dreams could ever conjure. The fans who filled the Coliseum, the Paramount Theatre, the exhibition outposts, and today the heavenly Rose Garden. The fans who turned on their TVs, radios, and Internet connections, who bought the newspapers and the merchandise. Who lined the streets and flooded the squares, malls, and airports in loving and endless admiration, adoration, respect, and gratitude.

The fans who regularly gave and occasionally withheld their love and support as the true gauge of how we were doing—both on and off the court of dreams.

The fans. The BlazerManiacs. The loyalists who filled Memorial Coliseum for 18 straight years—still an NBA record, by far. The fans who painted themselves and brought their signs of encouragement and inspiration to the games. The fans who left offerings on my front porch—the more creative and imaginative, the bigger the game. The flowers, the food, the music, and so much more. They sustained us with these gifts of life. The fans who brought my bike back when I needed a ride home from the championship parade. They took us to unimaginable heights, never letting us down, never letting us get tired—of anything. If only we could have done more in return.

And they are still there today—forevermore, for everything.

Which makes it all so special and unique to be a Blazer.

Which is what this book and this party are really all about.

The never-ending game, season, tour, and party—it's all the same. Yes, we've rearranged their faces and given them all other names, but it still says "Blazers" on the jersey, on our foreheads, and in our hearts.

And this book captures it all so perfectly—as only Wayne Thompson can in print, along with the timeless, classic photos that take you there and back. Wayne Thompson. Someone who has been there every step along the way as really no one else has. Wayne Thompson—like the Blazers and this book—basically better than perfect.

Better in the way that they have shaped, molded, changed, and left our lives and world.

Leaving us with the satisfaction of accomplishment, achievement, happiness, and the success of the truest champion—that of the human spirit.

Because it is this spirit that drives us, challenges us, focuses and shapes us with the most powerful emotions—pride and loyalty.

Pride. Developed, nurtured, and built over 40 years. Pride. What makes us stand so tall and straight. And has us ringing the chimes of freedom from the top of Mt. Hood and shouting, "I'm with those guys. Let's go. What's next? We want more!"

And loyalty. Loyalty—the human attribute and personal characteristic that enables us to achieve extraordinary feats. Because we care.

I care. And I'm proud. That's why this has meant everything to me. It has been and is my life. I—like so many others—played my best here. I wish it could have been better and more. But like this epic masterpiece, it's what it is—life and life only.

Once again, we are in the game, on the bus, in the locker room, in the huddle. And the fans are standing. Cheering. Driving that train.

I am honored, privileged, and humbled to still be a small part of something so very special here in Portland, Oregon.

If the first 40 was this spectacular, imagine what the next will be.

If only Lewis and Clark could see us now. I know it's a lovely view from heaven, but I'd rather be here with you.

In the immortal words of Bill Schonely, who the NBA themselves tapped to put it all in perspective, as he let it fly one more time, the thunder rumbling from his billowing lungs, throughout the heavens:

I LOVE THIS GAME.

Bill Walton
Portland Trail Blazers 1974–79
Hall of Fame 1993

(above) Bill Walton christens teammates
and city dignitaries at
the championship celebration.

INTRODUCTION

When future historians look back on the milestones that marked the state of Oregon's progress and prosperity during the 20th century, they'll be taking names. The legends will include those men and women who made a difference by building things, inventing things, creating jobs, devoting their energies to charity, and generally helping shape Oregon's social and economic character.

And Harry Glickman's name will surely be on that list. A sports icon and pioneering promoter, Glickman, you see, accomplished something other notable Oregonians did not achieve in all their fruitful lifetimes—giving Oregon a national market identity. He is the man who single-handedly brought major league basketball to Oregon.

He is Mr. Trail Blazer, delivering the enterprise that has helped spur growth in all economic sectors, because that's what major league cities do. That it almost didn't happen is a story about how fate intervenes, with one man's perseverance, and what can happen when destiny calls.

Fast-forward to the second generation of Blazer history. You will see in those years the importance of team owner Paul G. Allen to the success of the Blazers brand, both on and off the court. He is a big part of this story, too. He's the man who may not have founded the Blazers, but kept them here through his financial support, his commitment to excellence in the people he hires, and his sheer love of the game.

❀

But first, here's the story about how the Blazers almost never came to be. In January 1970, the NBA expansion committee, meeting in Philadelphia, raised the franchise price to $3.7 million, causing a group of 10 local investors to back out, thus leaving Harry Glickman all alone, with no financial support to make it happen. Once back in Portland, Harry got a call from Seattle SuperSonics general manager Dick Vertlieb, who said he knew a guy who might be interested in staking an NBA franchise. That guy was Herman Sarkowsky, a Seattle homebuilder and, ironically, Glickman's wife's former brother-in-law. When the two met later, Sarkowsky made it clear that he was not interested in sharing the ownership with 10 Portland investors, but that he would be willing to put up all the money if he could interest two other friends of his, Larry Weinberg of Los Angeles and Robert Schmertz of New Jersey, in joining him.

When the league's February 4, 1970, deadline to select its new teams rolled around, Glickman still hadn't heard from Sarkowsky. So, armed with only a scheme to persuade the league's board of governors to accept Portland, a desperate yet still optimistic Glickman went to Los Angeles, in the hope that a good-faith offer would work. However, once he was in the hotel room of Abe Pollin, the owner of the Baltimore Bullets and the chairman of the expansion committee, the mood changed. A few members of the expansion committee, led by Ned Irish, the founder of the New York Knicks and a promoter of events at Madison Square Garden, didn't want Portland in the league. "How can I," Irish asked his fellow owners, "put the name 'Portland Trail Blazers' on the marquee of Madison Square Garden?"

Glickman left the room dejected. As he reached the lobby of the Beverly Wilshire Hotel, with the distinct feeling that his NBA dream had failed, he remembered that he had left his raincoat, a useless garment in sunny LA, back in Pollin's room. "When I got there," Glickman recalls, "Pollin was on the phone: 'Harry, it's for you . . . some guy named Sarkowsky is on the line.'" That was destiny calling.

Sarkowsky told Harry that he had reached Weinberg, who was eager to buy into an NBA franchise, and that he had finally gotten in touch with Schmertz. "Schmertz is in—we're set," Sarkowsky said.

So the birth of the Trail Blazers came down to the fact that in February a raincoat is an essential accessory in water-soaked Oregon, but is completely unnecessary in LA. That Harry Glickman forgot it on his way out of town is clearly, in the telling of stories, where fate intervened and destiny began for the Trail Blazers.

❀

Once back in Portland, there was much for Glickman to do—hire a staff, hire a talent scout, hire a coach, hire a publicist, hire a radio announcer, and select a team—all before the NBA college draft in March and the NBA expansion draft in May.

When I first learned that I would be covering the team on its maiden voyage, the organization had four employees, all of whom were drafted from Harry Glickman's Portland Buckaroos in the Western Hockey League. The group included business manager George Rickles; Edith Salkeld, a do-it-all office manager; a secretary, Mildred Harris; and John White, a seasoned newsman and former executive sports editor for Portland's *Oregon Journal*, who also served as the Oregon correspondent for *Sports Illustrated* and a stringer for *Time* and *Fortune*.

The day I first met John White at the team's tiny offices on SW Yamhill Street, he was sitting at his desk with a pile of papers and books partially blocking his view—a Damon Runyonesque throwback from the early 20th century who would be comfortable if William Howard Taft were president.

"Hi, Mr. White, I'm Wayne Thompson of the *Oregonian*, and I've been assigned to cover the Portland team this season."

(opposite, left to right) Commissioner Walter Kennedy, Harry Glickman, and Oregon Gov. Tom McCall at the inaugural game.

"THE BEST EXECUTIVE IS THE ONE WHO HAS SENSE ENOUGH TO PICK **GOOD** PEOPLE TO DO WHAT HE WANTS DONE, AND **SELF-RESTRAINT** ENOUGH TO KEEP FROM MEDDLING WITH THEM WHILE THEY DO IT."

—THEODORE ROOSEVELT

Looking up at me over his horn-rimmed glasses, White said, "I know who you are, Thompson. Why would the *Oregonian* assign a general-assignment reporter with no sports background to cover a major league basketball team? What's your angle?"

"I'm here because I'm probably the only guy over there willing to travel for six months a year," I replied sarcastically. Truth is, this was a dream job for me. I saw my first NBA game, between the Boston Celtics and the Baltimore Bullets, in 1950 at the age of 14.

As it turned out, White and I spoke the same language about basketball, newspapers, and many other things.

Through its first 40 years, Portland has been one of the league's most successful franchises; since 1971, only two other NBA teams (Los Angeles and San Antonio) have made more playoff appearances than the Trail Blazers. Portland also had a record run of playoff appearances—21 straight years, from the 1982–83 season to the 2002–03 season—a feat exceeded by only two other professional sports teams, the 1950–71 Syracuse-Philadelphia NBA franchise and the St. Louis Blues of the NHL.

The Blazers have a rich history, ably kept all these years by Chuck Charnquist, who played a major role in organizing the Trail Blazer picture file for this book and helping me remember what happened when. Chuck is the team's quintessential stats guy, the man to whom members of the Portland news media turn whenever a Blazer milestone is in the making. You want to know who scored Portland's first basket? Go ask Chuck. You want to know who missed Portland's last shot last year—or any year? Go ask Chuck. Over the history of the franchise, Charnquist has become the team's institutional memory, its historian, and its keeper of flames gone by.

You will see in the pages of this book what team owner Paul Allen has meant to the growth of the franchise and, indeed, to its salvation. A cofounder of Microsoft in 1976, Allen bought the Blazers from Larry Weinberg in 1988. The following season, 1989–90, Allen's team went all the way to the NBA finals before losing to Detroit, four games to one. His teams have posted an impressive 1,046–816 record in his 22 years as the Blazers' owner. Through most of those years, the Trail Blazer franchise has been the envy of the basketball world, mostly due to Allen's willingness to do whatever it takes to bring another NBA championship to Portland.

He built the 20,000-seat Rose Garden, which opened in 1995, added the league's most modern and efficient practice facility, has paid top dollar to his players, and has flown them around the country in his own private jet.

The possessor of an intuitive mind for basketball talent, Allen has a long history of accumulating star players and hot-prospect draft choices. The Blazers never lose players for financial reasons.

Within the context of telling the Blazer story, I should perhaps include my own brief introduction: I am an NBA fan for 60 years, a Trail Blazer fan, a reporter, and a live witness to 2,010 of the 3,788 games the Blazers have played. Having seen my first NBA game in Bangor, Maine, in the fall of 1950, four years after the NBA's predecessor league, the Basketball Association of America, was formed, I had the distinction of seeing Bob Cousy, Larry Bird, Magic Johnson, Kareem Abdul-Jabbar, Kobe Bryant, and LeBron James play as rookies, as well as seeing 75 percent of all the basketball players who are in the Naismith Memorial Basketball Hall of Fame, including Wilt Chamberlain, Jerry West, and Oscar Robertson, play in person.

As you will see throughout this book, the Blazers have had many more ups than downs. Their greatest coaches (Lenny Wilkens, Jack Ramsay, Rick Adelman, Mike Dunleavy, Nate McMillan) have guided them on the court, while their greatest general managers (Stu Inman, Bucky Buckwalter, Geoff Petrie, Bob Whitsitt, Kevin Pritchard) have kept them armed and dangerous through drafts, trades, and free agent signings.

You will find in following this chronicle that the greatest Blazer teams fall into four distinct eras 1974–81, 1988–94, 1997–2003, and, of course, the current Blazers, who have been on the rise since 2007, achieving a 33-win improvement in the standings in just three seasons.

I hope the fresh anecdotes, vignettes, and old game stories will stimulate a true Blazer fan's memory, and a chapter discussing the forty greatest players in franchise history, including the top six—Clyde Drexler, Bill Walton, Terry Porter, Geoff Petrie, Maurice Lucas, and Brandon Roy—as selected by a panel of Trail Blazer writers and historians, will start a few friendly arguments.

This is, of course, a coffee-table book, so if the text doesn't jog your memory of the Blazers' first 40 years, certainly the hundreds of images supplied by the *Oregonian*'s Bruce Ely and the newspaper's staff, combined with those from the Trail Blazer archives, clearly should.

Portland fans love their Blazers, as evidenced by the fact that from April 5, 1977, until November 20, 1995—814 games over a stretch of more than 18 years—the Blazers played to capacity crowds. That's a real testament to a fan's love of team, one that has never been matched by any other franchise in professional sports.

And this book comes not only as a memento of the first two scores of Trail Blazer history, but also at a time when the Portland franchise was once again a contender for an NBA championship.

"Rip City, all right," chants Bill Schonely, the longtime voice of the franchise, as he looks back on the Trail Blazers' exceptional body of work.

"It's a great day to be a Blazer," swoons broadcaster Brian Wheeler after every Portland win as he looks forward to the future.

What happens next has always been a hidden treasure—and one to be discovered when you least expect it.

(opposite) Contact sheet of coach Jack Ramsay, assistant coach Jack McKinney, and a flight attendant, taken by Bill Walton aboard a team flight in 1977.

ARE OFTEN THE
BEGINNING OF
GREAT ENTERPRISES."

—DEMOSTHENES

CHAPTER 1

IN THE
BEGINNING

> # "PERFECTION IS ATTAINED
> # BY SLOW DEGREES;
> # IT REQUIRES THE HAND OF TIME."
>
> —VOLTAIRE

When the Trail Blazers began their National Basketball Association journey—**October 16, 1970**—the nation already believed in miracles. Just a year earlier, America had put a man on the moon, so anything seemed possible, including a major league sports franchise for a small-market West Coast city such as **Portland**.

In 1970, only Salt Lake City of the rival American Basketball Association and Phoenix of the NBA had smaller metropolitan populations than Portland—west of Green Bay, that is.

"What's the odds of that happening?" asked Harry Glickman, the man most responsible for landing the franchise. "About the same as the moon shot," mused Herman Sarkowsky, the Trail Blazers' first owner.

Just a week before Portland made its regular-season NBA debut against the Cleveland Cavaliers, the Blazers made a deal. They sold one of their expansion picks—a veteran reserve guard—to the Los Angeles Lakers. His name: Pat Riley.

Looking back today, the early Blazer years clearly belonged to a another century—a time when the U.S. surgeon general worried more about the ingredients in aspirin than about whether Americans smoked or drank too much. Two of the twelve original Blazers (Gary Gregor, Ed Manning) smoked cigarettes. Gregor smoked my brand, so we based a relationship on bumming smokes. Jim Barnett and rookie Ron Knight occasionally smoked a cigar. Many of the Blazers drank beer regularly; some even openly frequented bars for the harder stuff. One of the Blazers—Stan McKenzie comes to mind—had his own key to Hugh Hefner's Playboy Clubs. Blazer players in those days did enjoy a night off in the great metropolises of the East.

Richard Nixon was president when the Trail Blazers were born. And even though the Vietnam War was raging and political assassinations were etched painfully on our collective psyches, people begged for tension relief. That probably explains why *Marcus Welby, M.D.*, one of the blandest sitcoms ever to grace the airwaves, was America's favorite television show. Simon and Garfunkel's "Bridge Over Troubled Waters" was the year's Grammy-winning tune, suggesting that we could all use a sedative. And in the same vein, Jim Barnett's favorite song was "Cracklin' Rosie" by a fresh new crooner named Neil Diamond.

(above) Rick Adelman, the first Trail Blazers captain.
(opposite) 1971 draft picks Sidney Wicks and Charlie Yelverton get their gear from trainer Leo Marty.
(previous spread, left to right) Sidney Wicks, Ron Knight, Willie McCarter, Gary Gregor, Walt Gilmore, Larry Steele, and Jim Marsh at fall camp in 1971.

Barnett, who scored the first Blazer field goal in the opening exhibition game against the Golden State Warriors at Longview, Washington, was the source of great entertainment during that magical first season. On long bus rides between Cleveland and Buffalo (the Blazers played the Cavs and Braves six road games each in that first season), Barnett would climb into the overhead luggage rack and take a nap.

One could say that 1970 was a rebuilding year for the nation, which was desperately searching for the calm after the psychedelic storms and protests of the turbulent '60s. It was the beginning of the polyester decade, of leisure suits, turtleneck sweaters, metal medallions, and long mink coats for long, tall basketball players. Of the inaugural Blazers, Stan McKenzie was the team's fashion plate, but Barnett, Knight, Manning, Gregor, and Leroy Ellis also sported knee-length furs.

The players loved them, but Barnett, according to Dale Schlueter, gave his badly shedding, knee-length rabbit fur coat to a homeless man who was begging for money on one of Chicago's frigid winter nights. "I know you'd rather have a shot of whiskey," Barnett told the man, "but take my coat—you'll thank me in the morning."

Let's face it—1970 produced crazy, zany times for the fledgling Blazers, who mellowed out over seven months of ups and downs in the knowledge that the people in their world didn't expect much.

The Blazers generally ignored bad news in those days. Only their brilliant rookie guard, Geoff Petrie, a graduate of Princeton, could be seen reading a newsmagazine—and his weekly of choice was *U.S. News & World Report*.

The young Blazers were having fun, posting a 29–53 record, the best of the three expansion teams (Buffalo and Cleveland were the others) that came into the league that season. Under coach Rolland Todd's "shoot first, ask questions later" offense, the Blazers were fun to watch. They were fourth in the league in scoring (115.5 points per game) and second in the league in shot attempts (104 per game), which meant that usually the first guy who was open after the ball passed the midcourt line let it fly.

But that's getting ahead of the story.

§

(above) Dale Schlueter, at 6-foot-10 welcomes rookie Bill Smith, the Blazers first 7-foot player, during 1971 media day.
(opposite) Blazers veteran center LeRoy Ellis shares a ball with Wendy Buel as Mrs. Sy Rodakowski looks on.

When Harry Glickman began to build his staff, fate and destiny also had a hand in that, too. First things first. He quickly needed to hire a personnel director to scout talented players. The college draft was just a month away. He got a tip from Seattle SuperSonics general manager Bob Houbregs that Donnis Butcher, a former player and coach for the Detroit Pistons, would be a good hire for that job. But just as he was about to call Butcher, Glickman's phone rang. It was Art Johnson, a promoter friend from San Francisco who called to say that he'd found the man Portland was looking for. Johnson said that Stu Inman, a former player and coach at San Jose State, knew more about the game of basketball than anybody—a testimonial seconded 37 years later by the legendary Bobby Knight in a column by the *Oregonian*'s Brian Meehan.

After hiring Inman on February 20—"the best decision I ever made," Glickman said later—he turned his attention to selecting a nickname for the team. One of the nicknames the new owners of Portland Basketball Inc. considered was the Chinooks, in recognition of the Chinook salmon, the prize fish of the Pacific Northwest, whose struggle for survival has been one of the great environmental stories of the last two centuries. But can you imagine all the bad jokes we'd be hearing today about a team named after an endangered species? Instead, Glickman wisely launched a name-the-team contest that received more than 10,000 responses from fans. The franchise later settled on the name Trail Blazers to honor the 18th-century pioneers who trail blazed the Oregon Territory.

"HE IS A GREAT PLAYER,
AND A GREAT SCORER
WHO CAN ONLY HELP
ME PLAY MY GAME . . ."

—SIDNEY WICKS, ON GEOFF PETRIE

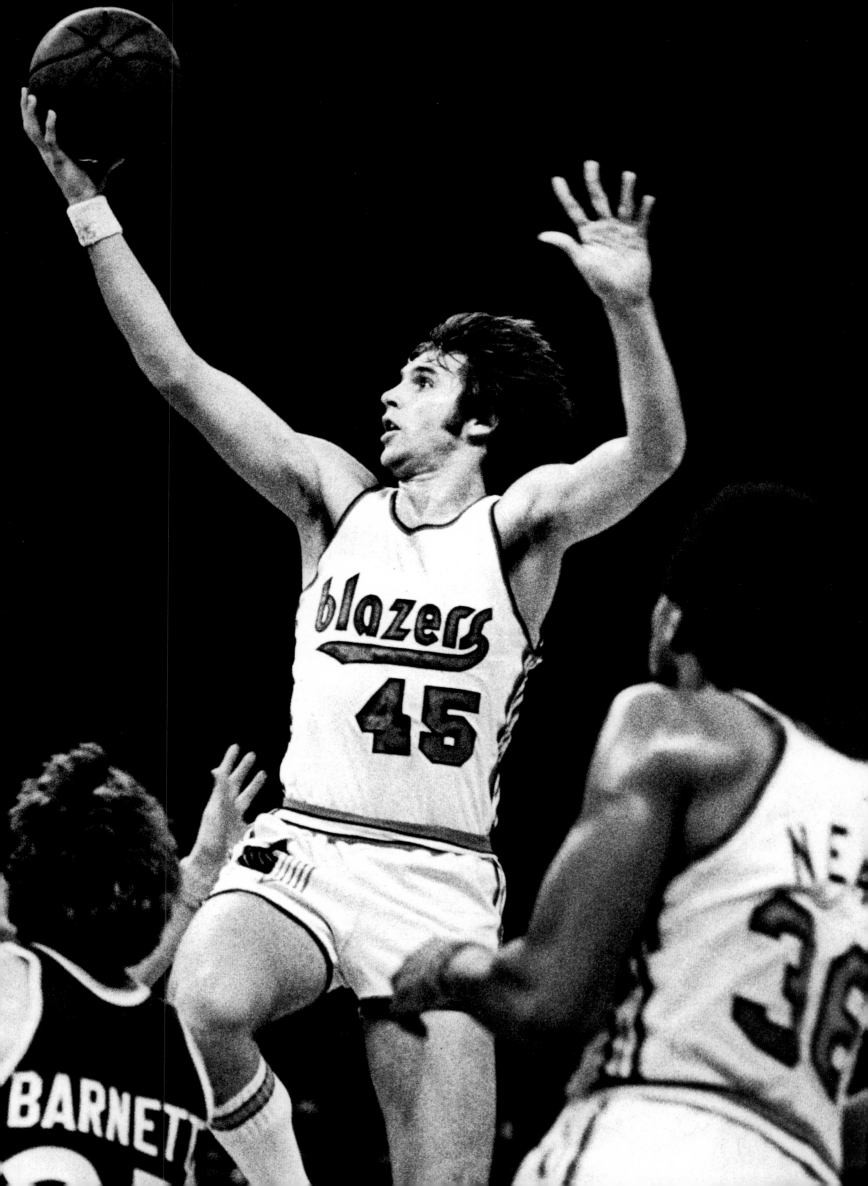

Once the nickname was set, a logo was chosen. It's been described as a pinwheel, a modern graphic interpretation of five players on one team playing against five players from another. Pretty basic stuff, but visually effective nonetheless.

Soon after, Glickman selected a coach, young Rolland Todd from the University of Nevada at Las Vegas (UNLV), on a recommendation from Inman, who got the tip from his close friend Pete Newell, the famed former coach at Cal. In those days in Portland, word-of-mouth endorsements from trusted sources were better than résumés. Todd promised a fast-breaking, free-shooting, hip-hop-before-hip-hop kind of basketball that would be really fun to watch. And he delivered on that pledge as the Blazers shocked the basketball pundits with wins over big-name, established teams—Baltimore, Atlanta, Chicago, Detroit, Boston, Seattle, San Francisco, the defending champion New York Knicks of Ned Irish, and the new 1971 champion Milwaukee Bucks—while also leading the league in shots missed.

To tell the Portland story to Blazer first-nighters and to sell the NBA game to skeptical Oregonians, Glickman chose Bill Schonely, a hockey and Major League Baseball broadcaster from Seattle, as the voice of the Blazers. And Schonz, in one way or another, has been that Blazer voice and goodwill ambassador ever since.

To all the sports pitchmen who came before—the Harry Careys, Mel Allens, and Red Barbers of the world—this must have been a match made in Hall of Fame heaven. Schonely has pipes that Frank Sinatra would admire. Not only is he beloved by generations of Trail Blazer fans, he also has the respect of all the players and coaches, past and present.

And even if he hadn't been a major force in introducing the Blazers to the fans, Schonely would still be known as the man who created "Rip City." It happened accidentally, in a first-season game against the Lakers. With Portland in the middle of a second-quarter rally, Jim Barnett swished a long jump shot—probably a 3-pointer if the rule had existed in those days—and out of Schonely's mouth came "Rip City—all right!" At the next time-out, Schonely's scorekeeper, Jeff Wohler, nudged him. "Hey, where did that come from?"

Schonz responded, "I don't know—it just came out."

"Well," said Wohler, "leave it in."

To this day, Glickman says his two best hires in that first year were Inman, who picked the team and later picked most of the players on the championship team of 1976–77, and Schonely, who brought the fans in.

(above) Jim Barnett scored Portland's first-ever point, as well as provided hours of off-court amusement for teammates.
(below) Rolland Todd teaches his young team the advantages of a shoot-first-and-often offense.
(previous spread) Geoff Petrie, a great shooter from any distance.

The Blazer rookie camp that first season resembled a casting party for a James Cameron extravaganza. After Portland's college and expansion drafts that summer, Stu Inman opened a tryout camp for anyone who thought he was good enough to make the Blazers' roster. It was crowded with wannabes looking for work as bit players in the NBA. More than 60 aspirants showed up for an afternoon of scrimmages at Memorial Coliseum.

Among the undrafted players were twins Floyd and Lloyd Kerr, who had been stars two seasons earlier at Colorado State; Nick Jones from Oregon, who played a couple of seasons in the ABA and later played with the Warriors; dozens of high school, junior college, and small-college players, none of whom had had a diet soda, let alone a cup of coffee, with a professional team's scouts at any level; and who knows how many kids whose only flirtation with basketball was playing a pickup game of H-O-R-S-E in gym class.

As it turned out, Inman selected four of his draft choices for the final team from that event—the first Blazer, Geoff Petrie; Walt Gilmore of Ft. Valley State, Georgia; Ron Knight of Cal State, Los Angeles, who would lead the Blazers in the rookie game with 34 points; and Claude English of Rhode Island. Joining these four to form the opening-day roster were Rick Adelman, LeRoy Ellis, Ed Manning, Stan McKenzie, and Dale Schlueter. Inman acquired Jim Barnett and Gary Gregor during the preseason and traded for Shaler Halimon after the season started.

In contrast to Buffalo and Cleveland, Portland's team featured a bunch of no-names, and, as far as the media was concerned, Portland was the worst of the three expansion teams. In fact, *Sports Illustrated* editors called the 1970 Blazers "the worst expansion team ever assembled in league history."

That they ended up with a better record than both the Braves or the Cavs, winning 16 of the 24 games against them, was a tribute to Inman's skill at finding hidden treasures among the less heavily scouted players and Todd's ability to turn this group of outsiders into a run-and-shoot circus.

A young fan unfurls a sign reading "Rip City," the signature name originated by Blazers broadcaster Bill Schonely during the team's first season.

The very first regular-season game, October 16, 1970, against the Cavaliers at Memorial Coliseum, was a very special night indeed. The Blazers were optimistic about the team they had chosen for the battle. The then governor of Oregon, Tom McCall, himself a towering 6-foot-5, but a man who never played or followed basketball along his path to political stardom, tossed up the ceremonial first jump ball. It barely cleared the outstretched arms of 6-foot-11 Cleveland center Luther Rackley and 6-foot-11 Blazer center LeRoy Ellis. People laughed.

McCall was joined at the opener by Portland's mayor, Terry Schrunk, and NBA commissioner J. Walter Kennedy, who quickly abandoned a position of neutrality; by halftime, he was rooting for the Blazers. Asked about it afterward, he said, "I spent my honeymoon in this town some 30 years ago, so there is a fondness in my heart for Portland." (Kennedy promised to root for the Cavs at their home opener the following week.)

The Blazers needed all the applause they could get from Kennedy, McCall, and Schrunk because the opening game drew only 4,273 fans. They may have been Oregon's only major league team, but during that maiden season, the Blazers had to win fan loyalty the hard way.

Because it was the Blazers' first game, two players achieved milestones. Jim Barnett, a former star at the University of Oregon and now a radio and television voice of the Golden State Warriors, scored Portland's first point 2 minutes and 42 seconds into the first quarter. He finished with a game-high 31 points. Ron Knight, a 6-foot-7 rookie, scored the Blazers' first field goal 53 seconds later. Ironically, he was to score only one other basket during the game. "That doesn't matter," Knight said years later. "I scored the first-ever Trail Blazer basket, and nobody, no time, can ever beat that record."

The Cavaliers led throughout most of that inaugural game as the crowd watched politely. Cleveland coach Bill Fitch took notice: "I thought it was a lively audience, if the sport they were watching was golf," he quipped. Later that season, Fitch was to gain fame when he described the poor turnouts at the Cleveland Arena by saying, "Hey, our crowds are good. It's just that half of them come disguised as empty seats."

After trailing for three quarters, the Blazers finally erupted midway through the final quarter as Blazer rookie Geoff Petrie finally found the range. With the Blazers trailing 102–96, Petrie, who had been held to 4 points in the first half, scored 6 points in a 20-second flurry and Portland was back in the game. Petrie, who finished the game with 21 points, scored again to draw the Blazers to within 2 points, at 106–104. Then Stan McKenzie stole the ball from Cleveland's John Warren and scored the tying basket with 4:02 remaining.

Seconds later, it was Petrie again, hitting a 15-foot jumper that woke up the tepidly appreciative gallery and began converting them to Trail Blazer basketball. The game story in the *Oregonian* the next morning claimed that Petrie's hoop "won the soul of the first-nighters," but in hindsight that was a bit of an overstatement. Following a free throw by Cleveland's Len Chappell, Barnett applied the capper, first with a 20-footer, then with another bomb from the corner, and finally with a driving layup with 14 seconds left, as the Blazers notched their first-ever victory, 115–112.

There were many heroes in that first Blazer victory 40 years ago. McKenzie had 19 points; Ellis had 15 points, 22 rebounds, and 5 blocked shots; and Ed Manning, the father of future NBA star Danny Manning, had 15 points and 10 rebounds in a 36-minute performance off the bench.

The debut of major league sports in Portland didn't reveal much about what kind of team the Blazers had, other than the notion that Cleveland wasn't very good either. It was clear, though, that this team would be fun to watch on offense, because it had so many players anxious to prove they belonged in the Show. Their first big chance to prove that came December 20, 1970, a day when time stood still for the Trail Blazers. They were leading the Philadelphia 76ers, 123–121, with one second remaining on the clock, the Sixers with the ball. All-Star 76ers guard Archie Clark received the inbounds pass. He faked left, took a dribble right, and then hoisted up a high-arching jumper from 27 feet away. When the ball finally came down, tickling the chords as it dropped through the rim, the horn sounded to save Philadelphia and send the game into overtime, which the 76ers eventually won, 134–132. It was said to be the longest second in Blazer history.

Of all the games the Blazers played in 1970–71, this one endures the test of time in that people still remember it and can recite what happened in that last long moment. For Rolland Todd, this game tarnished what was otherwise a successful season. At the team's 1980 reunion, Todd made this point: "I always tell people that we won 30 games that first season. I will always count that Philly game as a win."

(above) Harry Glickman (left) and co-owner Herman Sarkowsky (on phone) were chiefly responsible for the birth of the Blazers.
(opposite) Larry Steele was a third-round draft choice out of the University of Kentucky.

Trail Blazer fans in 1971 were just learning how to pace themselves in rooting for a team that played 82 games over six months during a mostly dark and damp season. The second-year Blazers were very young—their average age was 23.8 years old—and frankly not very good. And six months is a long time to grieve when your team loses four out of every five games. Nevertheless, fans, being fans, have expectations. Absent steady victories, they cling to the little things, the special moments. And the Blazer road game at Detroit on December 7, 1971, proved to be one of those special moments. It marked the long-anticipated return of Geoff Petrie, the 1970–71 co–rookie of the year, adding firepower to the starting lineup, alongside that season's prized rookie, Sidney Wicks.

Petrie was coming off preseason knee surgery following a sensational rookie season in which he averaged 24.8 points per game. He was one of only three guards

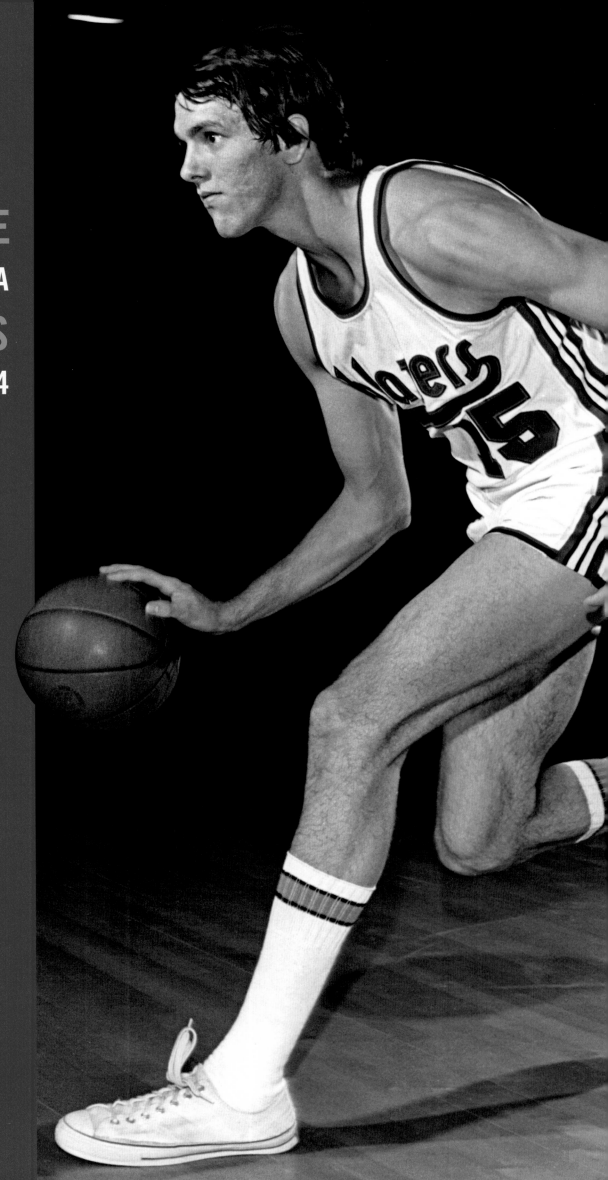

STEELE
IN THE NBA
IN **STEALS**
IN 1973–74

in NBA history to score more than 2,000 points in his rookie season (Oscar Robertson and Michael Jordan are the others). Wicks, in his rookie year, almost matched Petrie, averaging 24.5 points per game.

(Today, with 2,031 points as a rookie, Petrie ranks eighth all-time, behind Wilt Chamberlain (2,707), Walt Bellamy (2,495), Kareem Abdul-Jabbar (2,361), Michael Jordan (2,313), Bob McAdoo (2,261), Oscar Robertson (2,165), and Rick Barry (2,059). Wicks is the ninth player on that list, with 2,009 points in his rookie year.)

Sidney Wicks was either the greatest forward in Trail Blazer history or one of the more disappointing, depending on how you weigh his supreme athleticism and potential against his self-prescribed days off. An All-American at UCLA, he was a cinch to become the No. 1 player in the 1971 draft. In a surprising move, the budget-conscious Blazer ownership paid Cleveland $250,000 to take Austin Carr with the first pick, paving the way for the Blazers to select Wicks. When he arrived in Portland to negotiate his contract, he said he wanted a $1 million deal. Weinberg and Herman Sarkowsky, who were both smart about money, replied, "Fine"—then gave him his million dollars at the rate of $50,000 a year for 20 years.

There was no question about Wicks's talent. He led Portland in scoring in three of his five seasons. He still holds the franchise record of 27 rebounds in a game, and ranks fifth in career rebounds and ninth in scoring. According to Lionel Hollins, whose rookie year with Portland was Wicks's last season, "Sidney was the prototype of power forwards today. He was big, could run the court, shoot, post up, pass, put the ball on the floor—he could do it all as a player, and he played hard." Today, Petrie says, "Sidney was a unique blend of power, speed, and quickness. He was also was a pretty good passer for a frontcourt player."

In the eyes of most professional basketball pundits, Petrie and Wicks constituted the finest young one-two combination in the league—arguably a firm foundation on which to build a winning franchise. But would the Petrie and Wicks duo make the Blazers more competitive right away—or ever? Would the two potent scorers, each driven by a shoot-first, pass-later mentality, play in harmony? Those were questions yet to be answered as the Blazers, who had lost 21 of their first 25 games that season, landed in Detroit.

When the two budding superstars were asked about how they felt about playing with each other, this is what they said:

Wicks: "I welcome Geoff with open arms. He is a great player and a great scorer who can only help me play my game, instead of me having to assume so many other responsibilities."

Petrie: "With Wicks on the floor, there's always somebody to go to. It takes the pressure off me and makes opponents play an honest defense. Teams won't be able to risk stacking their defenses with Sidney around."

The Petrie-Wicks show, on that day in Detroit at least, fulfilled all expectations and then some. In 44 minutes, Petrie connected on 16 of 22 floor shots and added four free throws for 36 points. Four of his five assists set up Wicks for layups. Wicks, in turn, drilled 13 of 25 shots and four free throws for 30 points, and tied center Dale Schlueter with a game-high 16 rebounds. All three of Wicks's assists set up Petrie jumpers.

Before he was a Portland Trail Blazer, Terry Dischinger was an All-American at Purdue, a member of the 1960 U.S. Olympic Team (the first "Dream Team" that included Jerry West, Oscar Robertson, Jerry Lucas, Darrell Imhoff, and Walt Bellamy), and the 1963 NBA Rookie of the Year for Chicago.

A PRESIDENTIAL GUEST

BY WAYNE THOMPSON

In the fall of 1974, the nation was convalescing from the wounds of Vietnam and Watergate and adjusting to a new president, Gerald Ford. Meanwhile, the National Basketball Association was beginning its 28th year, oblivious to the political climate outside its buildings. So when President Ford came to Portland on November 1, 1974, to stump for Republican political candidates in the general election, not too many Trail Blazers were paying attention. That changed the night the Blazers played the Buffalo Braves with the president of the United States in attendance. By basketball standards, it wasn't an extraordinary game. The Blazers, with some late-game heroics, won it, 113–106.

A former football player at Michigan, Ford liked spectator sports, and while he wasn't an autograph-seeking fan, he told aides that he was interested in seeing Bill Walton play. And like most politicians, he knew which team to root for. Several times during the game, Ford displayed emotional reactions when calls went against the Blazers. In those days, Walton was neither a fan of the political establishment nor a fan of the Republican Party. Nevertheless, he acknowledged to writers after the game that seeing the president of the United States sitting behind the Blazers' bench invoked a surreal feeling.

Wicks, Portland's leading scorer with 27 points, was one of the few Blazers who wasn't especially pleased by Ford's visit. "It's a heavy trip to see these FBI guys come in and push people around," Wicks said. "But it didn't bother me. I've seen presidents before."

While the Blazers kept their cool under the pressure of playing before the president, their statistician apparently didn't. He came up two field goals short during the time when Ford and his party were sitting directly behind him.

Later, at the Benson Hotel, the president, sleepless in Portland, came down from his room wearing pajamas and a dressing gown, and joined a private after-hours party hosted by White House photographer David Hume Kennerly. "That Blazer game really worked me up," the president told Kennerly's guests.

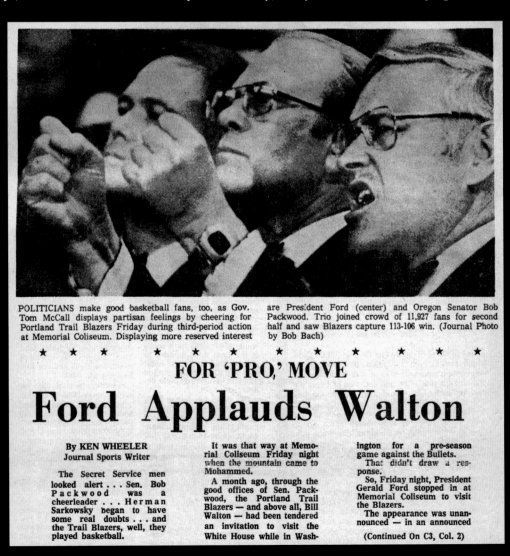

POLITICIANS make good basketball fans, too, as Gov. Tom McCall displays partisan feelings by cheering for Portland Trail Blazers Friday during third-period action at Memorial Coliseum. Displaying more reserved interest are President Ford (center) and Oregon Senator Bob Packwood. Trio joined crowd of 11,927 fans for second half and saw Blazers capture 113-106 win. (Journal Photo by Bob Bach)

★ ★ ★ ★ ★ ★ ★ ★ ★ ★ ★ ★

FOR 'PRO,' MOVE
Ford Applauds Walton

By KEN WHEELER
Journal Sports Writer

The Secret Service men looked alert . . . Sen. Bob Packwood was a cheerleader . . . Herman Sarkowsky began to have some real doubts . . . and the Trail Blazers, well, they played basketball.

It was that way at Memorial Coliseum Friday night when the mountain came to Mohammed.

A month ago, through the good offices of Sen. Packwood, the Portland Trail Blazers — and above all, Bill Walton — had been tendered an invitation to visit the White House while in Wash-

ington for a pre-season game against the Bullets.

That didn't draw a response.

So, Friday night, President Gerald Ford stopped in at Memorial Coliseum to visit the Blazers.

The appearance was unannounced — in an announced

(Continued On C3, Col. 2)

Clipping from the *Oregon Journal* November 2, 1974

Yet despite these heroics, the Blazers had to rely on the play of their supporting cast to pull off a 131–130 upset overtime win. This was not among the greatest games in the Blazers' memory book, but it also was not a harbinger of the stormy Petrie-Wicks era to come.

For Petrie and Wicks, this unlikely Blazer invasion of Cobo Arena was the most significant road victory they'd get in what was otherwise Portland's most humbling NBA season ever—18 wins, 64 losses.

The rivalry between Petrie and Wicks, despite its happy beginning, didn't take long to become nasty. On December 30, 1971, two months into Wicks's rookie year, Portland lost 117–92 at Chicago. Wicks, who had 23 points and 14 rebounds, told Bill Schonely that he wanted to be the postgame radio guest, at which time he unloaded his frustrations. "We degenerated into a group of individuals tonight and never resembled a team," Wicks told Schonely. "We played like it was just a pickup game in a high school gym. Guys just wandered on and off the court and never gave up the ball. Everybody out there is playing for themselves, and it stinks. Some people are playing team ball; some people aren't. We're out there getting the crap kicked out of us by teams we can play with. There are too many guys dribbling with their heads down and not looking for others."

The media took Wicks's comments to be directed mostly at Petrie (now president of basketball operations for the Sacramento Kings). So did Petrie, who the following

day was quoted as saying, "Twice [when I took shots], he [Wicks] just stood there and shook his head like he should have had the ball. I ran around for six games and never saw the damn ball. Now, all of a sudden, he doesn't think he's getting it enough? He is just as guilty as anyone else. We have all chiefs and no Indians. Something has to be done, or we won't win another game all year."

After the 1971–72 season, Inman and his wife, Eleanor, took Petrie, Wicks, and their wives on a trip to Israel. It was the brainstorm of co-owner Larry Weinberg, who hoped it would cement a better relationship between the two stars. What followed was a scene that could have been lifted from a parable about Cain and Abel. Petrie saved Wicks's life in the Sea of Galilee, of all biblical places. The group had gone out for a swim when Wicks found himself in peril. "Sidney got cramps in both of his legs and started calling for help," Petrie says. "He wasn't far out, and I got him to shore. He coughed up a lot of water. Finally, he said, 'Thanks a lot. I'm too young to die.'"

Despite all that drama, their relationship on the court and off it never jelled—though neither player would admit it, then or ever. Their games simply didn't mesh. To fulfill their potential, they both needed to be the go-to guy, with 20 or more shots per game, and, despite their denials, they just didn't warm up to each other—the Sea of Galilee incident notwithstanding. And so, when coach Jack Ramsay arrived in the summer of 1976, both of them were traded, Wicks to Boston and Petrie to Atlanta.

(opposite) The Trail Blazers' first play-by-play announcer, Bill Schonely, first coach, Roland Todd, and first player, Geoff Petrie. (below, left to right) Bill Walton, Sidney Wicks, and agent Sam Gilbert at the 1974 press conference announcing Walton signing with the Blazers. (right) Coach Jack McCloskey and assistant coach Neil Johnston, the Blazers' first assistant coach and a Hall of Fame player for the Warriors.

One of the most memorable Blazer games of this era was the opening game of the 1974 season—Bill Walton's rookie year. Entering their fifth NBA season, the Trail Blazers were ecstatic about their prospects. The June draft that brought them UCLA All-American Walton was the talk of the town.

After suffering through four losing seasons while their beloved team compiled a league-worst 95–233 record, Trail Blazer fans chirped throughout the summer about making the playoffs for the first time, rather than handicapping next year's draft selections.

Fans in the Rose City were just convinced that Portland had a powerhouse club, on paper. The basis of that optimism was this:

• Portland had firepower with two of the top 10 scorers in the league in Sidney Wicks (23.6 points per game) and Geoff Petrie (23.5 ppg). And it had versatile small forward John Johnson, who had a career scoring average of 16.4 ppg.

• The Blazers had a new coach, Lenny Wilkens, who had decided to add one more season to his Hall of Fame credentials as one of best point guards ever to play the game by playing for the team, too. Nobody knew back then that Wilkens would be inducted into the Hall of Fame as both a player and a coach.

• And, of course, they had the remarkable Mr. Walton, the component they had been missing all along—a big-time, major league center to combat the likes of Kareem Abdul-Jabbar, Nate Thurmond, Bob Lanier, and Bob McAdoo.

So, at the opening ceremonies for the game versus Cleveland in Memorial Coliseum on October 18, 1974, the crowd of 11,409 was abuzz with enthusiasm.

At first, the game didn't live up to its billing. Both teams had been off for a week and were rusty. Despite what Blazer fans regarded as an awesome starting five—Wicks, Johnson, Walton, Petrie, and Wilkens—the Blazers shot only 39 percent to take a scant 44–40 halftime lead.

The second half saw the Cavaliers rally in the third quarter, then fall back in the fourth, until Bobby "Bingo" Smith canned a long jumper to give the Cavaliers a 97–95 lead with 13 seconds left.

That's when Bill Walton, as he had done so often at UCLA, made a move to the hoop and was fouled with six seconds left. In those days, when a team was in a bonus-foul situation, a player who was fouled while shooting got three chances to make two free throws. Walton made the fans sweat by missing the first one, but he swished the next two to send the game into overtime.

Until then, the Blazers, in their short history, had never won an overtime game, but Wilkens reminded his troops that he had played for teams that had won many OT games. And Walton pointed out that he had never lost one. Wilkens, then 36, thrived on pressure, but he wasn't expecting to play this kind of role in the last year of a fabled 15-year NBA career.

Nevertheless, Wilkens played 60 minutes against the Cavs—"about twice as long as I expected to be out there," he said afterward. "But the coach in me said that we needed what Lenny Wilkens the player could provide in the way of leadership and experience."

In the end, it was not Wilkens or Walton, both of whom fouled out, but Wicks and Petrie who provided the Blazers with the game-winning heroics. After both teams battled bucket for bucket through the first three overtime periods, it looked again like this game was destined to be tied forever. With 77 seconds remaining on the clock in the fourth overtime and the score tied, 127–127, Wicks tipped in a missed jumper by Petrie. Sixteen seconds later, Wicks stole a Cleveland pass that Petrie converted into the game-winning jumper.

Portland had prevailed in this marathon, 131–129, so Blazer fans went home happy, convinced that their team was going to stir up trouble for opponents in the NBA.

They were content in the knowledge that their new coach/point guard had scored 15 points and dished out 10 assists.

They were overjoyed that their rookie center's debut had produced 18 points and 24 rebounds.

Player-coach Lenny Wilkens, assistant Tom Meschery, and the oft-injured Bill Walton during the 1974–75 season.

They were thrilled that Walton's backup—the much-maligned LaRue Martin—had contributed 10 points and 11 rebounds in 22 minutes.

For John Johnson, who scored 29 points and snared 11 rebounds, the four-overtime win was special for a couple of reasons: Like Wilkens, his coach, Johnson was a former Cavalier who enjoyed beating his ex-teammates, and he was celebrating his 27th birthday that night. After a long, hot shower, Johnson reappeared at his locker in the Blazers' dressing room, still smiling. "This is a helluva note," he said, checking his watch. "The overtimes pushed this game past my birth date, so I won't have any time to celebrate it." The game lasted three hours and seven minutes, making it at that time the longest game in Trail Blazers history.

Statisticians didn't know back then that Wilkens would become the winningest coach in NBA history (surpassed by Golden State's Don Nelson during the 2009–10 season), so they weren't counting. But this was win No. 122 for Wilkens, who amassed 1,332 victories in 32 seasons.

The next season, Wilkens tried to persuade the organization to trade Wicks. If they had listened to him, perhaps he would have become the coach of Portland's only championship team. Despite all the summer talk about making the playoffs, though, fans of 1974–75 Blazers would have to wait two more seasons to see their team make it to the Promised Land, and they learned a lesson in the process:

Teams don't win championships on paper.

🌀

As the Blazers open their 41st season and begin their fifth decade, that very first step for Blazer-kind in 1970 seems quite distant and insignificant compared to the hunger today for another NBA title.

When that first Trail Blazer game was played, millions of today's Blazer fans throughout the world were yet to be born. Others were in various stages of learning how to walk, talk, and get along in life when the *Oregonian* proclaimed that Petrie's shot had won the soul of the Trail Blazer first-nighters.

Some 40 years later, those Blazer hearts and souls are still up for grabs, each and every night.

🌀

Coach Lenny Wilkens (right) with ABA transplant and future Blazers broadcaster Steve Jones.

TRAIL BLAZERS' NEMESIS

BY WAYNE THOMPSON

If you were to ask Trail Blazer fans to name the best players Portland ever faced, their list would probably include Kareem Abdul-Jabbar, Nate Archibald, Charles Barkley, Larry Bird, Kobe Bryant, Wilt Chamberlain, Julius Erving, George Gervin, Lou Hudson, LeBron James, Michael Jordan, Magic Johnson, Bob Lanier, Karl Malone, Moses Malone, Pete Maravich, Bob McAdoo, Shaquille O'Neal, Oscar Robertson, and Jerry West.

My vote would go to Wilt "the Big Dipper" Chamberlain. By any accounting measurement you want to take—statistics or wins and losses—he was clearly the most dominant opponent the Blazers ever faced. As a member of the Los Angeles Lakers, Chamberlain played 16 games against the Trail Blazers over three seasons, 1970–73, averaging 19.2 points, 19.4 rebounds, 5 assists, and 8 blocked shots per game.

He rarely missed a shot in those 16 games. In six games against Portland in 1972, Wilt connected on 35 of 42 field goals, including 21 in a row. He holds the NBA record for once making 35 field goals in a row.

One of the funniest scenes in Blazer history happened on December 6, 1970, in the L.A. Forum, when Blazer guard Jim Barnett, at 170 pounds, crawled up on the 285-pound Chamberlain's back and rode him downcourt, like the proverbial gnat on a Brahma bull's back. Wilt didn't seem to notice at first, but then, as if to say, "If you hurt me and I find out about it, there's gonna be hell to pay," the big man just flexed his left shoulder, spilling Barnett to the floor.

When a great sports figure passes, the tendency with all of us is to cut to our own personal highlight film stored away in memory. For Joe DiMaggio, I see his graceful stride in catching up to a fly ball; for Secretariat, it is his runaway gallop at the Belmont; with golfer Payne Stewart, it's the clothes.

My highlight film for Wilt begins on a snowy night in the parking lot of Memorial Coliseum. Some kid throws a snowball at Chamberlain, and he catches it and throws it back. That is intimidation. That is dominance. That is the way Wilt Chamberlain played in Portland.

Wilt Chamberlain toys with 6-foot-10 Blazers center Dale Schlueter during a 1971–72 Lakers game.

"EVERYBODY PULLS FOR DAVID, NOBODY ROOTS FOR GOLIATH."

—WILT CHAMBERLAIN

THE
BIRTH

OF
BLAZERMANIA

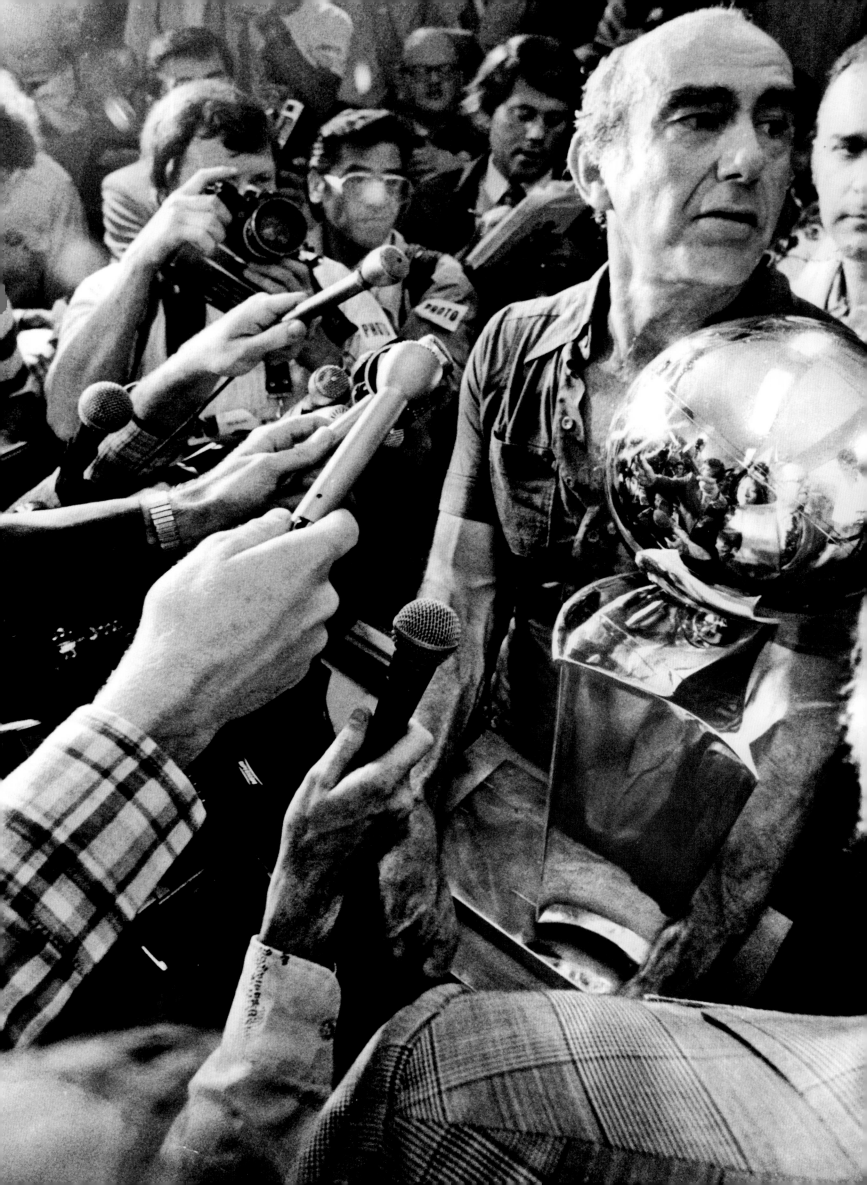

"SPORTS DO NOT BUILD CHARACTER— THEY REVEAL IT."

—HAYWOOD HALE BROUN

The Trail Blazers' road to the championship in the 1976–77 season was uncannily like the plot of the movie *Rocky*— both stories feature an underdog going the distance against enormous odds.

(opposite) Coach Jack Ramsay, holding the Championship Trophy, shares a special moment in Blazers history.
(above) Corky Calhoun joins in the post-game celebration.
(previous spread) Coach Jack Ramsay celebrates the Blazers' championship.

As the Blazers prepared for their seventh NBA season, a relatively unknown actor named Sylvester Stallone was making his way to glory on the big screen.

The comparisons are striking: The movie won the Academy Award for Best Picture in the same year that the Trail Blazers, cellar dwellers in the Pacific Division, began their miraculous run to their first and only NBA title in their first-ever playoff appearance.

For moviegoers, the sight of a sweaty Rocky Balboa charging up those 72 steps in front of the Philadelphia Museum of Art was uplifting, a personification of the American dream. So, too, was the sight of the young Blazers dousing one another with champagne in their locker room after achieving their own improbable dream, a dramatic come-from-behind victory over the heavily favored Philadelphia 76ers for the NBA Championship.

Local writers were having a field day trying to describe the sudden outbursts of ecstasy popping up all over town. Author, teacher, and former professional baseball pitcher Larry Colton put it in perspective, though, by showing the enormous significance of the event, as perceived by Blazer fans, when he wrote, "It was the first time Portland had made the national sports news headlines since Neldon Driggs won the indoor fly casting championship in 1947."

All sarcasm aside, this really was a very big deal for Portland and Oregon: It was the birth of a brand—Trail Blazers basketball—that helped establish a national-market identity. Finally, people could distinguish Portland, Oregon, from Portland, Maine.

The seeds of the Trail Blazers' national brand were planted long before the bloom, dating back five years to the 1971 NBA college draft, when Portland's visionary talent scout, Stu Inman, selected Larry Steele of Kentucky in the third round. In 1972, Inman got Dave Twardzik of Old Dominion (who had initially signed with the Virginia Squires of the ABA) and Lloyd Neal of Tennessee State in later rounds as well. These players had been overlooked by most NBA scouting systems.

In the 1975 draft, Inman selected Lionel Hollins of Arizona State as the sixth pick of the first round (predictable) and Bob Gross of Long Beach State, the 25th pick in the second round—another major coup.

Steele, though, was one of Inman's all-time best picks. He wasn't a star at Kentucky, but he was a starting guard for a major power.

Even though Steele averaged only 8.2 points per game in nine seasons as a Blazer, his name still stands out in the record books, and his single-game exploits still remain a big part of the team's oral history, passed down from generation to generation.

Steele led the NBA in steals (217, for a league-leading 2.68 average per game) in 1973–74, the first year that the league officially kept that statistic. The following season, on November 16, 1974, at Memorial Coliseum, Steele recorded 10 steals, tying the record set by Jerry West. His thefts also established the all-time Blazer record (later tied by Clyde Drexler and Brandon Roy), helping Portland beat the Lakers, 112–99.

That game also may have been Steele's greatest single moment as a Blazer. He came within one assist of becoming the only Blazer in history to record a quadruple-double—12 points, 11 rebounds, 10 steals, and 9 assists. His remarkable defensive achievements, however, are not what most Blazer fans over 40 remember about Steele. They remember the Shot.

It happened on January 28, 1979, at Memorial Coliseum in a game in which the Blazers routed the Philadelphia 76ers, 116–94. With just seconds left in the third quarter, Steele took an inbounds pass at Portland's end of the court, turned, and let loose a two-handed set shot from 80 feet away.

Swish! It was the longest field goal ever made by a Blazer.

Later that summer, Steele was invited to speak to a group of kids at a basketball camp at David Douglas High School. The first request asked by a camper was, "Show us how you made that shot." After the talk, Steele went to the baseline of the gym and threw up a one-hander. Swish!

(above) An intense Jack Ramsay (left) and assistant coach Jack McKinney watch playoff action in 1977.
(opposite) Blazers Lionel Hollins, Larry Steele, Bill Walton, Johnny Davis, and Dan Anderson labor through the "Ramsay Mile" in 1976 fall camp.

The startled campers cheered with glee, but Steele, tongue-in-cheek, turned to them and simply said, "It's really not that difficult a shot."

Steele's game was full-court-pressure defense: floor burns, lane-filling fast breaks, and constant running to torment opponents.

Taking Bill Walton of UCLA with the first pick in the 1974 draft didn't showcase Inman's gift (finding the unheralded player is where he excelled), but even if you didn't want a star player who drank carrot juice and ate broccoli pie, Bill Walton was a lock, even if he was a load. He also was the greatest passing big man—and perhaps the most unselfish one—the NBA has ever known. During his years with Portland, Walton average 4.41 assists per game, topped only by Wilt Chamberlain's 4.44 among NBA centers all-time. (Chamberlain's statistical edge came from the two seasons, 1966–68, in which he concentrated on leading the league in assists.)

At UCLA, (1971–74), Walton became a basketball legend as the Bruins won the national title in 1972 and again in 1973, with an 87–66 win over Memphis State in which Walton made an impressive 21 of 22 field goal attempts and scored 44 points. Some regard this as the greatest offensive performance in American college basketball history. (Walton actually connected on 24 of 25 field goals in that game, but three of them were disallowed on offensive goal-tending calls.) He was the backbone of two consecutive 30–0 seasons and was also part of UCLA's record 88-game winning streak. Walton's personal winning streak lasted almost five years. His record at UCLA was 86–4. Add to that his high school record of 74–1 at Helix High School in La Mesa, California, and you get the picture. Bill Walton was an all-time winner.

Many fans were so ecstatic that the Blazers won the right to choose the Big Redhead, as he was called back then, that the team's season-ticket sales soared twofold over the previous year. They just knew he was one of the greatest centers ever. And they were proven right in 1996, when a panel of basketball experts named him one of the NBA's 50 greatest players of all time.

In his injury-shortened four seasons with the Blazers, Walton was content, for the most part, to let his teammates—Geoff Petrie, Sidney Wicks, Maurice Lucas, and Lionel Hollins—do all the scoring. As one of the greatest all-around centers ever to play the game, Walton, somewhat surprisingly, was never the go-to guy on offense—more likely the second or third option in the half-court offense. For example, he was the Blazers' leading scorer in only 62 of the 209 games he played in Portland. His best regular-season game, while not a factor in the standings, came against the Atlanta Hawks—a 36-point, 22-rebound performance on January 11, 1976, as the Blazers beat the Hawks 116–109 in Atlanta. Like Bill Russell before him, Walton was the defensive stopper, the shot blocker and fast-break initiator who made the high-flying Blazers one of the most exciting teams to watch. Along with Wes Unseld, Walton could deliver the quickest and most accurate outlet pass—seemingly all in one twisting motion from the point of rebound to the overhead pass downcourt—that the NBA had ever seen. A devout fan of the Grateful Dead, the young Walton was also a vegetarian, wore flannel shirts, and carried his basketball clothes in an onion bag. His multicolored headbands wrapped tightly around his long, flowing, and sometimes ponytailed red hair made him look like a prototype of snowboarder Shaun White.

During his college days, Walton was jailed once for taking part in a Vietnam War protest. As a Trail Blazer, he remained a zealot for social causes, supporting Cesar Chavez's farm workers' movement and advocating freedom for American Indian Movement (AIM) defendants Dennis Banks and his wife, KaMook; Kenneth Loud Hawk; and Russ Redner. In May 1976, when U.S. District Court judge Robert C. Belloni dismissed with prejudice the government's firearms and explosives charges against the four AIM leaders, Walton and his roommates, Jack and Micki Scott, themselves implicated months earlier in the disappearance of the fugitive Patty Hearst, held a victory celebration party at Walton's northwest Portland home.

Attorney John Bassett, the person who knew Walton best in Portland and has remained his friend to this day, once told me, "Bill is a lot different than a lot of professional athletes. He loves basketball, but he cares about the world, too. He worries about people and our future as a nation, and he longs to do his part to right the wrongs he sees in life."

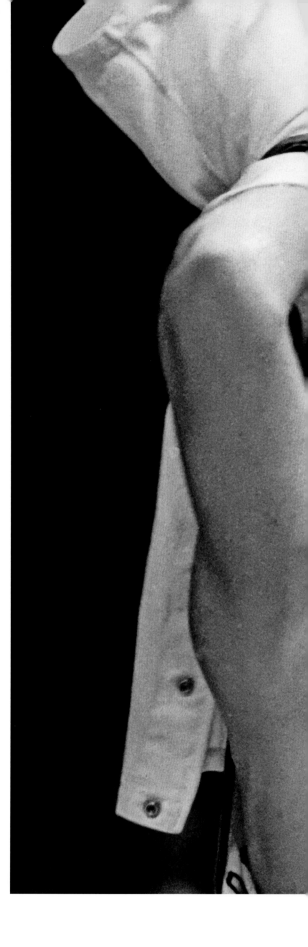

Stu Inman was lauded by his peers in those days for often seeing something in players that few others saw. He was revered for finding, in later rounds, undervalued and unscouted players (most of whom played for small schools, or had small roles at big schools). Examples: Larry Steele, Lloyd Neal, Dave Twardzik, and Bob Gross.

On the other hand, he also took the heat for sometimes blowing the first-round pick: LaRue Martin, Sam Bowie, Rich Laurel, Barry Parkhill, and, if you want to include wasted opportunities, Wally Walker. The Blazers could have gone for broke in 1976 and taken Adrian Dantley of Notre Dame with the fifth pick in the college draft, instead of choosing Walker.

Some of the criticism of Inman's high-level draft picks was unfair. For example, when he selected Martin, Chicago Loyola's center, with the first pick of the 1973 draft—a selection often regarded as one of the worst in NBA history—Martin was not the player Inman wanted. It turns out that Inman really wanted North Carolina All-American Bob McAdoo, a future Hall of Famer. And the Blazers thought they had him signed on the eve of the 1973 draft. Although all the small-print items had been agreed to at about four o'clock in the morning, McAdoo's agent came back five

The drafting of Bill Walton spurred a two-fold increase in ticket sales.

hours later with new contract demands for more money. When Harry Glickman phoned the Blazer ownership about the changes, Herman Sarkowsky told him to tell McAdoo's agent to "go to hell." With McAdoo out of the picture, the Blazers, over Inman's protest, decided to take Martin. It was not Inman's call, but he never told the media that.

A classic big-man matchup pitting Kareem Abdul-Jabbar against Bill Walton in the 1977 Western Conference Finals.

The most important move, however, in rebuilding the 1975–76 team, coached by Lenny Wilkens to a disappointing 37–45 mark, was hiring Jack Ramsay, who had guided Buffalo to the playoffs the previous three seasons, as head coach. It wasn't that Wilkens had been a failure as a coach; his tenure was marked by Walton's series of injuries and the problems he was having in convincing management to deal Sidney Wicks.

Ramsay, though, brought a fresh approach, emphasizing a running game that suited the Blazers' personnel, and with him came an able assistant in Jack McKinney. They had been longtime friends and colleagues in Philadelphia, and they shared a similar basketball philosophy.

Ramsay outlined his approach to coaching in his book *The Coach's Art*, cowritten with John Strawn:

> *What is this game that runs through my mind? It is a ballet, a graceful sweep and flow of patterned movement, counterpointed by daring and imaginative flights of solitary brilliance. It is a dance which begins with opposition contesting every move. But in the exhilaration of a great performance, the opposition vanishes. The dancer does as he pleases. The game is unified action up and down the floor. It is quickness, it is strength; it is skill, it is stamina, it is five men playing as one . . . . It is winning; it is winning; it is winning!*

Next, Portland traded popular Geoff Petrie, an original Trail Blazer, and center Steve Hawes to Atlanta in exchange for the No. 2 pick in the American Basketball Association dispersal draft. That brought to the Blazers 24-year-old power forward Maurice Lucas, who, like Rocky Balboa, fought opponents bigger than he was (Artis Gilmore, Darrell Dawkins, come on down!). The ABA draft also brought to the team an undisciplined and raw 20-year-old named Moses Malone. Malone remained a Blazer through the fall exhibition season but was traded to Buffalo five days before the opening of the regular season for a 1978 first-round draft choice and $232,000. Trading Mo, the Hall of Famer–to-be, was a big mistake, most basketball pundits opined. After Malone

collected 24 points and 12 rebounds in a 129–114 preseason victory over Seattle, Walton and Lucas lobbied hard for management to keep him. But it was too late. The Blazer brass had already sealed the deal to send Malone to Buffalo.

The Blazer management saw trouble brewing if they kept Malone. They argued that young Malone, who had been an emerging star in the ABA, would command a larger salary than they were willing to pay and also would demand playing time.

Inman reasoned that Ramsay would have a difficult time finding minutes for Malone behind Walton, Lloyd Neal, and free agent Robin Jones, whom the Blazers had signed in August. An unhappy Moses, it was argued, might not lead the Blazers out of the Pacific Division, let alone into the Promised Land. This argument was based entirely on speculation, of course. The Blazers would have been better off had they followed Walton's advice: "Never trouble trouble until trouble troubles you."

The liquidation of the ABA also gave Portland the chance to sign one of its former (1972) draft choices, Dave Twardzik, who had spurned the Blazers four years earlier and signed with the Virginia Squires of the ABA to be closer to his alma mater, Old Dominion. He had been a solid point guard with the Squires for four seasons and was just the kind of player Inman was looking for.

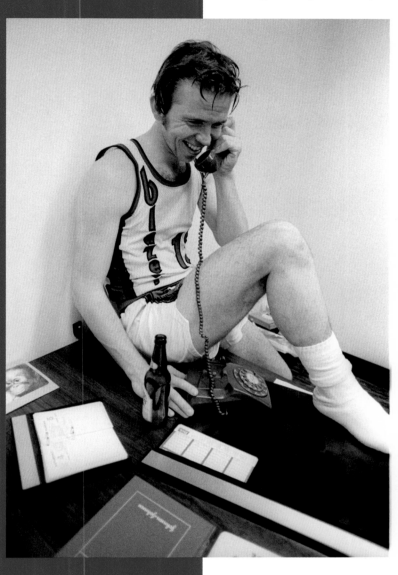

(opposite) Only one NBA coach can be identified by his colorful sideline wardrobe—the inimitable Jack Ramsay. *(above)* Guard Dave Twardzik takes a break from the post-game celebration to make a phone call.

Before the regular-season games began, the Blazers sent the high-scoring but difficult Sidney Wicks to Boston, acquired shooting guard Herm Gilliam from Seattle, and signed defensive specialist Corky Calhoun, who had been released by the Lakers.

That was the new roster of players who joined veterans Walton, Neal, and Steele and sophomores Hollins and Gross. But if you'd like to spice your dream team with a little what-if, consider how good the Blazers of 1976–77 and beyond would have been if you were to add future all-stars Moses Malone and Adrian Dantley to the roster (instead of Wally Walker). Regardless, the Blazers of 1976–77 were largely a bunch of no-names. Only Bill Walton had cover-story potential. ABA transplants Lucas and Twardzik got so little news coverage while playing in their defunct league that few NBA followers knew their true value. Walton himself hadn't heard of some of them.

For instance, the first day Twardzik showed up in the Blazer office, in the summer of 1976, he bumped into Walton, who was checking his mail. Later, Walton asked a secretary, "Who's that?"

"Dave Twardzik, from the ABA," was the reply.

"If he's been playing for four years in the ABA and I haven't heard of him, he can't be much," Walton said. Yet once Walton saw the firebrand Twardzik play, with his fearless drives to the basket and his seeming disregard for his own well-being, he became one of his biggest fans.

When this magical Blazer season got under way, none of the national publications gave the team a chance to make the playoffs, or even post a winning season. And the snub made sense. Who among the NBA's plentiful pundits would be so bold as to predict that the youngest team in the league—with a brand-new coaching staff and seven new players—would vault from last place to the championship in a single season? Even in a year when Seattle Slew, purchased at auction for a measly $17,500, won thoroughbred horse racing's Triple Crown, you wouldn't find many takers for these 100-to-1-shot Blazers.

Despite having 7 players on their 12-man roster who had never played together before, the Blazers started fast, winning 7 of their first 8 games and 16 straight at home before losing to the Lakers, 115–111 in overtime, on December 18, 1976. And they closed the season the same way they started it, winning 7 of their last 8. Like a lot of young teams do, however, they had yet to master how to win on the road. They were second in the league, with a 35–6 home record, but won only 14 of 41 road games, tying them with four other teams for seventh place.

Some writers credit a rookie, Johnny Davis, with making the difference in the playoffs. In Game 5 of the Denver series, starting guard Twardzik sprained his ankle. At that point, Coach Ramsay had two choices: move the veteran Steele to guard and thus maintain an experienced starting unit (Ramsay's usual MO: never trust rookies), or go with the 22-year-old Davis, who could provide speed and quickness to the offense and defense.

"Things changed instantly for us," Walton later wrote. "We went from being a very good team to an unbeatable one." In the final 11 Portland playoff games, Davis excelled on defense and averaged 13.1 points per game. His 25 points helped the Blazers eliminate Denver.

That was followed by Portland's stunning four-game sweep of the league's best regular-season team, the Los Angeles Lakers. An unsung star of the Laker series, who was single-handedly responsible for winning Game 2 in Los Angeles, 99–97, was little-used Herm "the Trickster" Gilliam, the least likely player in Ramsay's structured system to become a hero as Portland made its surprising run to a world title.

Buried on the Portland bench in Ramsay's pass-first, dribble-last and move-without-the-ball offensive system, Gilliam delivered what no other Blazer on that championship team could—instant offense. For about 10 minutes in the fourth quarter of Game 2, he became the best offensive player in Blazer history not named Clyde Drexler.

Down by 11 points in the third quarter and unable to combat the inspired inside play of Kareem Abdul-Jabbar, Ramsay turned to Gilliam, who turned the game around by taking the Laker guards to school. With a variety of arching jump shots, shake-and-bake spin moves, and dipsy-doodle floaters that he'd picked up over the years from watching his idols—Earl "the Pearl" Monroe and Pistol Pete Maravich—Gilliam scored 20 of his 24 points in the second half to ignite Portland's comeback. Quite simply, it was his defining moment as a player.

With Davis and Hollins in the starting backcourt, the Blazers were 9–2; moreover, they became a different team on defense as Davis and Hollins harassed opposing ball handlers with their foot speed and on-the-ball double-teaming tactics.

(left) Rookie guard Johnny Davis speeds around in the Blazers' productive pick-and-roll offense.
(above) Maurice Lucas clears the board in the playoffs' opening round versus the Bulls.

"When Johnny took over, we were able to pressure like crazy," Hollins says today. Indeed, defensive pressure set the tone for the sweep of the heavily favored Lakers in the Western Conference finals because it prevented guards Lucius Allen and Don Chaney from getting Kareem Abdul-Jabbar the ball as often as the Lakers would have liked. "Without Johnny, we don't sweep the Lakers that way," Hollins later told the *Oregonian*'s Jason Quick.

Even after surprising just about everyone with playoff wins over Chicago, Denver, and Los Angeles, the Blazers remained a dark horse with the bookies. Nevada sports books installed the Philadelphia 76ers as 13–10 favorites to claim the grand prize. Fans throughout the nation, looking at the star-studded Philadelphia roster, figured that a Sixer sweep of the no-name Trail Blazers was more than likely, if not inevitable.

Remember, this all happened before ESPN's *SportsCenter*, a program on cable TV that now allows fans throughout the country to discover the small-market teams that don't set their clocks to Eastern Standard Time. *Newsweek* sports writer Pete Axhelm, an astute observer of the national sports scene, provided a good explanation for why the 1977 Blazers were not getting the national respect they deserved. Just before the start of the Blazers-Sixers series, Axhelm wrote:

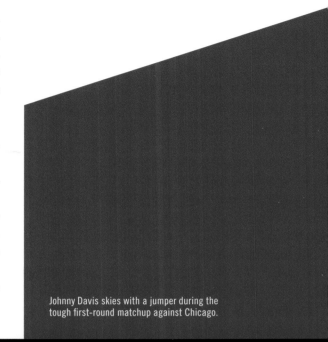

Johnny Davis skies with a jumper during the tough first-round matchup against Chicago.

> *The Trail Blazers are an intriguing team. Operating out of the Northwest far from the media glare of New York and California, they have performed many of their heroics too late to get them included in most of the country's newspapers. So fast guards like Lionel Hollins and Dave Twardzik have settled for being legends in their own time zone, and mighty Maurice Lucas has scarcely drawn a headline as he quietly surpassed George McGinnis and Julius Erving of the Sixers as the most effective forward in basketball.*

Frankly, the Blazers surprised themselves as well as everyone else. Their regular-season record of 49–33 was only third best in the Western Conference. And even that was padded by a 35–6 home-court mark, second best in the league. But they were a dismal 14–27 on the road. For all 12 of the 1976–77 Blazer players, NBA playoff basketball was an alien concept. Only Herm Gilliam had been to the playoffs before.

They were the youngest team (average age, 24.8 years) in the NBA that year, so it's little wonder, then, that they entered the championship round ignited by their own innocence. In fact, the team was so intoxicated by their sudden rise to the NBA's pinnacle event that they were oozing with confidence. And, thus they showed little fear of the highly favored Philadelphians, led by the great Julius Erving.

The playoffs, leading up to the finals, had been a great confidence builder for Portland—a relatively easy ride compared to what the Sixers had to do to get there (beating Boston, 4–3, ousting Houston, 4–2). Portland's surprising four-game sweep of the Lakers, who had finished the regular season with the best record in the NBA, really jump-started BlazerMania in Portland and gave the team nine days of rest. It got the nation's attention as well.

But when the championship series finally opened on Sunday, May 22, it was the Blazers, not the game-weary Sixers, who played as though they needed a rest. Nothing about Portland's running or passing game was crisp. Yet despite making 34 turnovers—that Philadelphia converted into 26 points—the Blazers kept the game close, behind Walton's 28 points and 20 rebounds, before losing out, 107–101.

One tactical surprise: Caldwell Jones, one of the few unheralded Sixers, proved to be a Blazer nemesis as Sixer coach Gene Shue used his 6-foot-11 center to bring the ball up the court, thus reducing the effectiveness of Portland's guard-oriented full-court traps.

Philadelphia steamrolled Portland in Game 2. The Blazers were simply awful, committing 29 turnovers and shooting only 35.6 percent from the floor. And the Blazers, no longer drunk on their own newspaper clips, had the right to be a little worried, because the Sixers simply outplayed them in virtually every phase of Game 2, winning handily, 107–89.

Blazer fans, meanwhile, were reminded by the media that no Pacific Northwest team had won a major league sports championship since 1917 (when Washington State College won the Rose Bowl), and it didn't seem like this squad would be the one to reverse the trend. Given those two lickings by the Sixers, one would think that on the Blazers' flight back to Portland, the players, facing their darkest hour, would start questioning themselves.

But there was one momentum changer that helped Portland regroup emotionally. Philadelphia's 20-year-old giant, Darryl Dawkins—perhaps the strongest man in the NBA—more or less body-slammed the smaller Bob Gross, then started swinging at him (he missed but accidentally hit his own teammate Doug Collins).

The ensuing melee ended only when Maurice Lucas, the Blazers' enforcer as well as their leading scorer, shocked Dawkins with an elbow to the head. The Sixers won the game, but the Blazers were invigorated. "That fight was a major factor," recalls Walton. "We were on the ropes. We were just not playing good basketball. Then Maurice stood tall and said 'Look—no one is messing with my team.'"

"It gave our guys a little shot in the arm," added Ramsay. "And then, before the third game began, Lucas ran over and shook hands with Dawkins, which really got our crowd all excited."

So on the way back from the City of Brotherly Love after the two disturbing losses, the Blazers were upbeat and seemed to thrive on being disrespected by the Philly fans and Mr. Dawkins, written off by the media, and told by all that they couldn't dig themselves out of this hole. When he was told that no NBA team had ever come back to win from two games down in an NBA championship series, Walton simply quipped, "You mean we'll be the first to do it. I like it."

Looking back on it, this third game against the Sixers was the real turning point of Portland's championship season—the watershed moment—even though generations of Trail Blazer fans might disagree. They have seen the film clip of the final seconds of their team's all-time shining moment—winning the NBA championship—dozens of times, on the Rose Garden's big screen, in reruns on TV, and, for some devout Blazer memorabilia collectors, on videotape or DVD.

Indeed, most Blazer fans, young and old, can recite those final seconds of Game 6 dribble by dribble. Here's a refresher: Philadelphia's George McGinnis takes a 15-foot jump shot with four seconds left. It bounces off the rim. Bill Walton leaps high to slap the ball toward center court, where Johnny Davis grabs it and runs out the clock. That prize moment in Trail Blazer history, when Portland bested Philadelphia 109–107 for all the marbles, is not unlike similar sports memories that fans throughout America cherish.

They serve society well as exercises in nostalgia. You know the type: Carlton Fisk coaxing his 1975 World Series home run into fair ground against Cincinnati; Michael Jordan's game-winning jumpers (pick one) against the Hoyas, Cavs, Jazz; the Miracle on Ice.

Reliving those precious milestones usually starts with the question "Where were you when . . . ?"

However, the question that Blazer fans could be asking in retrospect is not where they were when Portland won its first and only NBA crown, but where they were a week earlier, on May 29, 1977, when the Blazers faced the Sixers in Memorial Coliseum, down two games to none. For a young basketball team that many pundits believed had no chance—or, for that matter, no business—being in the finals against the multitalented 76ers, this was above all a psychological test.

To win the championship after being embarrassed in Philadelphia, the Blazers had to win four of their next five games. Not impossible, but not likely. So, as the Blazers flew back to Portland on May 27, they were in desperate need of moral support. And they got it at the airport where more than a thousand cheering Blazer fans, ignoring the Philadelphia massacres, were waiting to greet them at two o'clock in the morning.

As the Blazers prepared for Game 3, they faced some challenges: They had to sharpen up their passing game, control the boards, ignite their dormant fast break, and, most important, find some way to slow down Philadelphia's superstar, Julius Erving. The answers to some of those challenges came swiftly.

Sparked by Johnny Davis, the Blazers jumped to a 24–8 lead in the first eight minutes. Philadelphia did get back into the game, pulling to within 1 point at 54–53 with 1:28 left in the half, but the Blazers never relinquished the lead after that, although, with Erving scoring from all angles, the Sixers trailed by only 4 points, 91–87, early in the fourth quarter. That's when the Blazers pulled off arguably the most memorable eight seconds of basketball in the history of the franchise. This precious moment, like the one when Walton volleyed the ball to Davis in the final seconds of the championship game, started when Bob Gross spotted Walton cruising the baseline and lobbed a pass in his direction. Walton lost his balance in trying to reach the ball, but he did manage to tap it into the basket before crashing to the floor. With Walton down, the Sixers tried to create a five-on-four advantage up the court, but Dave Twardzik stole the inbounds pass and threw another lob toward Walton, who had just gotten to his feet. Same result: Walton slammed it in.

"BASKETBALL IS A FIVE-MAN GAME. THE BLAZERS PLAYED AS THOUGH THEY INVENTED THE CONCEPT."

—JULIUS ERVING

(above) Dr. Jack and his star pupil, Bill Walton, talk it over in the run up to the 1977 playoffs. (opposite) Walton was dominant on the boards in the final game against the Sixers with 20 points, 23 rebounds, and 8 blocked shots.

The double hoops by Walton in less time than it takes most people to get out of bed in the morning aroused a record Memorial Coliseum crowd of 12,923 and triggered a great fourth-quarter explosion on offense. Portland scored a record 42 points during the period, en route to a resounding 129–107 victory.

What was even more surprising than the final score, though, was that Portland had finally found a way to slow down Dr. J. He had 28 points through three quarters but was blanked by Gross and Corky Calhoun (with defensive help from their teammates) in the fourth period.

So, yes, the waning moments of the June 5, 1977, Portland-Philadelphia championship game may be what Blazer fans recall when they reminisce about the good old days. But, if truth be told, their beloved basketball team had it figured out a week earlier.

In Game 4, two days later, the Blazers jumped all over the Sixers, roaring to a 19–4 first-quarter lead as Lucas, Walton, and Hollins did all the scoring. Game 4 proved to be a statement maker, as the Blazers never let up, outscoring Philly 41–21 in the third period, on their way to a 130–98 romp. The series was even, 2–2.

Game 5, back in Philadelphia, where the media forecast another Sixer victory, was no contest either. It was a romp, all right, but it was the Blazers, using their superior team speed and rebounding, who crushed the Sixers, 40–25, in the third period, to take a 19-point lead. The 76ers staged a mild rally in the fourth quarter, but the Blazers' lead never was in danger as they claimed home-court advantage, 110–104, and a 3–2 series lead. This was their fourth win on the road in nine playoff games, giving the team more confidence that at last they had learned how to play their game away from home.

The Blazers' charter flight home, which landed at Portland International Airport at 4:30 a.m., Saturday, June 4, was greeted by more than 5,000 screaming BlazerManiacs. BlazerMania, by now, was delirious and seriously contagious. Both teams expected a war for Game 6 on the afternoon of Sunday, June 5.

(below) Fans were an inspiration in the Blazers' title run against Philadelphia. *(opposite)* Bobby Gross played tough defense in all six games against the great Sixers' forward Julius Erving and ran him to exhaustion at the offensive end of the floor.

And that's what the nation saw on TV. The lead changed hands a dozen times, and it was 40–40 five minutes into the second period when the Blazers exploded on a 10–0 run, finally taking a 67–55 lead into intermission. Erving, who had 40 points, but only 3 in the final quarter, and George McGinnis, who finally broke out of his series-long shooting slump with 28 points, kept the Sixers in the game. But each time the Sixers cut the Blazers' lead to within a few points, Portland had the right answers and pulled away.

With 20 points, 23 rebounds, 7 assists, and 8 blocked shots, Walton simply wouldn't let the Blazers lose the lead or the series. It was the greatest performance by a player in the deciding game of an NBA championship series ever, setting records for defensive rebounds and blocked shots. Another key to the victory was Gross, who ran Dr. J. into near exhaustion. Erving was magnificent, hitting 17 of 29 shots. But after chasing Gross around the court all day (Gross scored 24 points on 12 of 16 shooting), the Doctor made only 1 of 6 shots down the stretch.

The last 2:29 were agonizing for both teams. Portland led comfortably, 108–100, but could score only 1 more point (a Lucas free throw) for the rest of the game. The Sixers, meanwhile, missed three good looks at the hoop in the last 18 seconds, any one of which might have tied the game. The last of those shots—a 15-foot jumper by McGinnis—was short. As it hit the front of the rim, Walton leaped high in the air, tapping the ball toward midcourt to a speeding Johnny Davis as the clock ran down from the realm of fancy to become fact. The Blazers were champions of the world and the town went crazy, fans swarming the court to hug their favorite players; one guy climbed to the top of the backboard to get a better look at the wild scene below, and an exhausted Walton took off his shirt and slung it into the crowd.

"It's like when Mt. St. Helens blew its top," said Larry Steele. "People remember exactly where they were. Twenty years later, people were coming up to me and telling me exactly where they were and what they were doing when the Blazers won the championship."

"People ask me if I ever get tired of talking about that team," added Lionel Hollins. "No, I never do." While Walton and Lucas were Portland's stars, Ramsay's system didn't revolve solely around them. Ball movement, balance, and individual sacrifice were the Blazers' trademark. "Everything was about blending," Hollins recalls. "Give it up, get it back, give-and-go. It was basketball in its purest form. The guy who was open got the ball."

"There were egos, no doubt," wrote Eric Neel in a column entitled "Blaze of Glory," for ESPN, "but the squad was young (the youngest team to ever win an NBA title; Davis was just 21 years old, Hollins and Gross were 23, and Walton and Lucas were 24) and moldable . . ."

Even 20 years later, when the Blazers celebrated the anniversary of that series, the Sixers' players paid their respects to the champs but also lauded the team's selfless style and approach to the game. "The Blazers were blessed with unbelievably talented and intelligent players. That combination was what made them a great team," said George McGinnis.

The great Hall of Famer Dr. J added, "Basketball is a five-man game. The Blazers played as though they invented the concept. We were a team that possessed great individual, one-on-one skills, but Portland played like a committee, with no part greater than the whole. In the end, the team concept prevailed."

Henry Bibby, Philadelphia's starting point guard, said it best, though: "The Blazers of 1977 showed the sports world what an all-for-one-and-one-for-all attitude can achieve in a team sport. I've never seen an NBA team which played so much together, were so unselfish. All through their lineup they had guys who could run you ragged—Davis, Twardzik, Gross, Steele, Gilliam. They just moved without the ball so well, waiting for those great Walton passes.

"Say whatever you want about the way that series went. In my estimation, we couldn't have beaten that team," Bibby said.

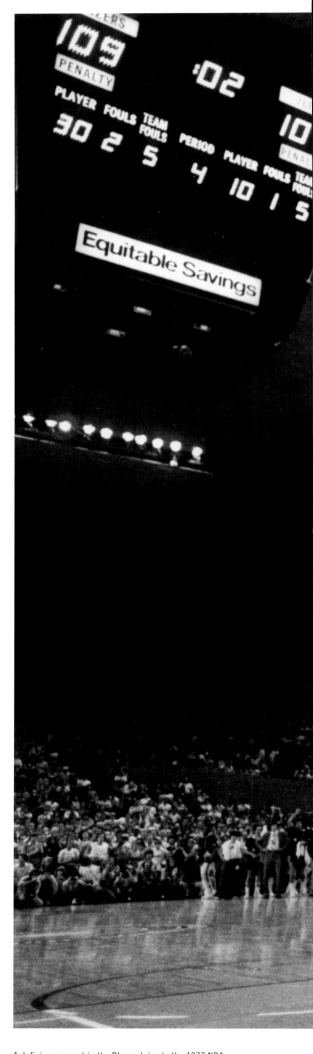

A defining moment in the Blazers' rise to the 1977 NBA Championship, when Bill Walton leaps high to slap a George McGinnis miss to Johnny Davis, who dribbles out the clock.

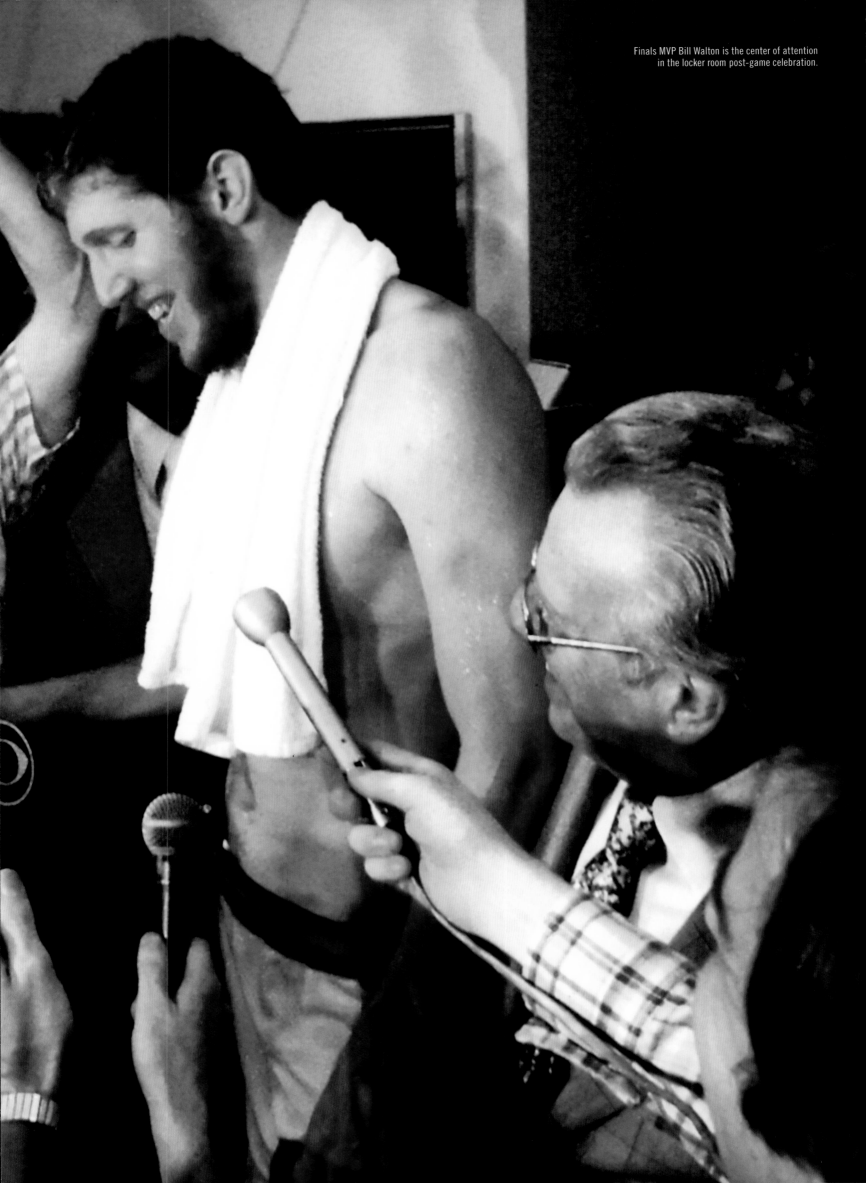

Finals MVP Bill Walton is the center of attention in the locker room post-game celebration.

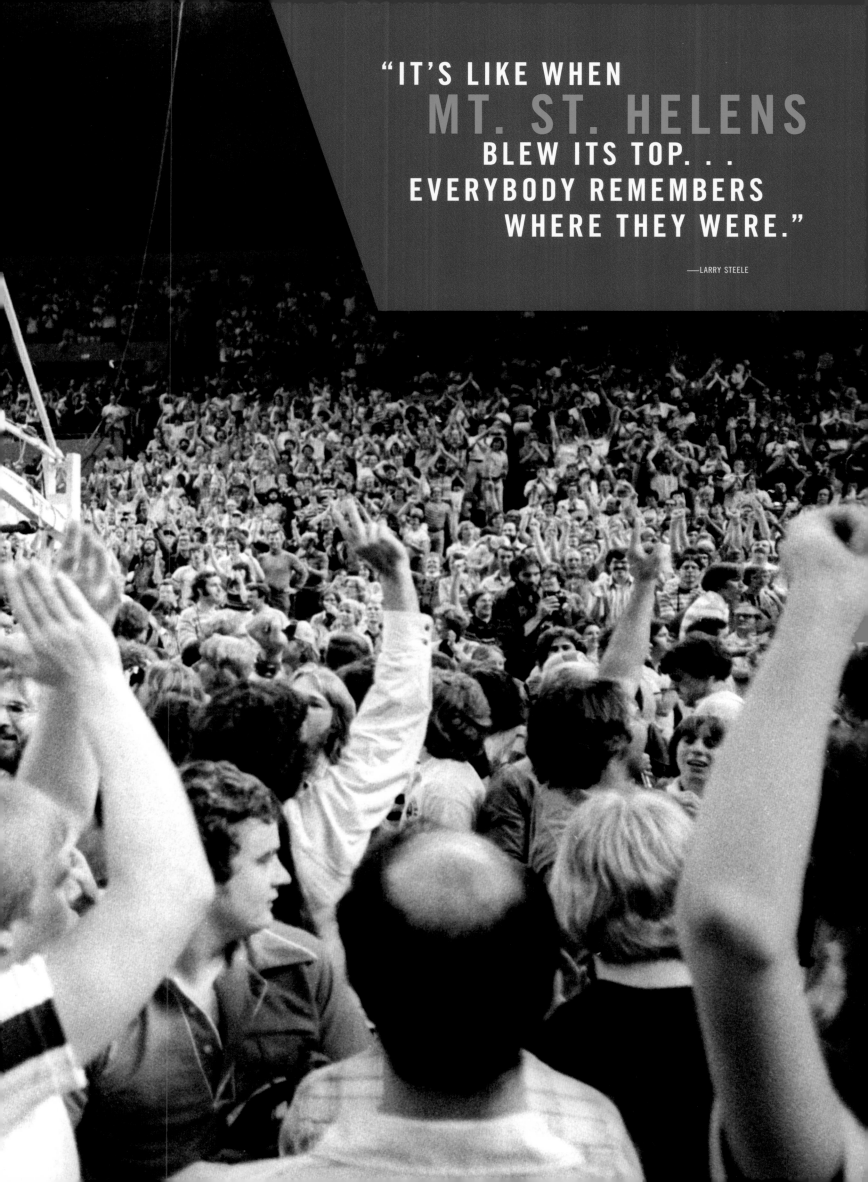

"IT'S LIKE WHEN
MT. ST. HELENS
BLEW ITS TOP. . .
EVERYBODY REMEMBERS
WHERE THEY WERE."

—LARRY STEELE

Every Blazer felt what Bibby said. "We were unselfish by nature, and we completely bought into Coach Ramsay's system and passing game," Davis said—and the players all saw the rewards of their unselfish style almost immediately.

When that final buzzer sounded at Memorial Coliseum at 2:18 p.m., it triggered one of the most spontaneous celebrations in Oregon history. The next afternoon, the Blazers were honored with a parade through downtown Portland. Police estimated the crowd at 150,000, but it has grown to at least twice that size over the last three decades as people who may or may not have been there now claim it as a bragging right.

For many fans, June 5, 1977, was a defining moment for Portland, Oregon, in terms of its market identity and their connection to it. Even today, decades later, the Blazer championship is still recalled as the sports highlight of the 20th century in Oregon.

And for Stu Inman, the architect of this beautiful team, the championship confirmed his belief—for all to see—that team character and selflessness are ingredients that can overcome raw talent.

For the whole team, despite their tender years and the long careers they had ahead of them, the championship season was their crowning achievement as basketball players.

(opposite) The scoreboard announces that the Blazers have become the 1977 World Champions. *(below)* Proud Fans of the 1977 NBA Champions. *(previous spread)* Fourteen-year-old Tom Zauner, perches on the rim to unhook the net during the championship post-game frenzy. Celebrating with him on the backboard is Dan Holden (standing).

Maurice Lucas reaches out to Sixers great Julius Erving as fans storm the floor.

A fan displays the front of the *Oregonian* with the headline "Blazers win!!!"

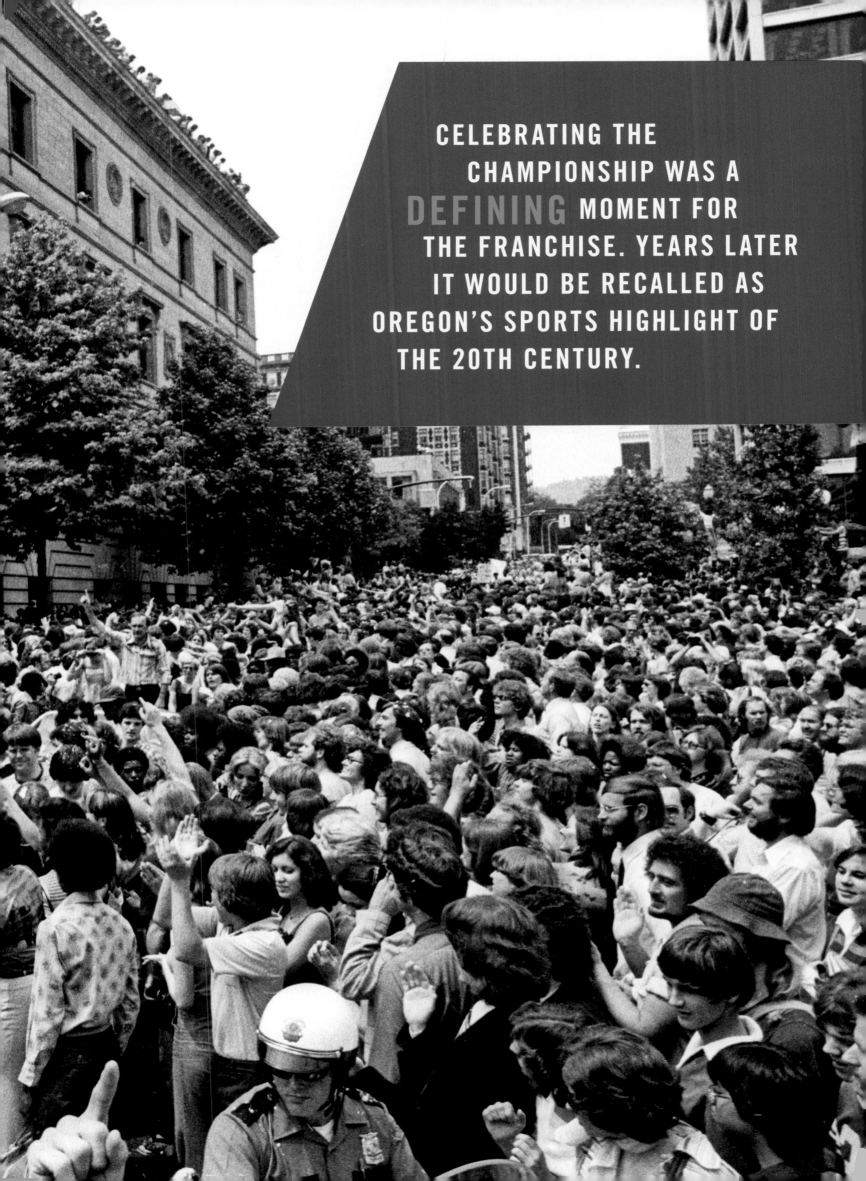

CELEBRATING THE CHAMPIONSHIP WAS A **DEFINING** MOMENT FOR THE FRANCHISE. YEARS LATER IT WOULD BE RECALLED AS OREGON'S SPORTS HIGHLIGHT OF THE 20TH CENTURY.

(opposite and previous spread) The crowd was estimated at 150,000 people for the downtown celebration, but that number has doubled in the past three decades as an increasing number of people now claim to have been there.
(above) Portland fans greet Dr. J as he leaves Memorial Coliseum in a show of respect toward their team's opponent.
(below) Bill Walton celebrates with the championship trophy.
(next spread) Coach Jack Ramsay leads the championship parade.

CHAPTER 3

THE
GREATEST
TEAM EVER

"BETTER A BROKEN PROMISE THAN NONE AT ALL."

—MARK TWAIN

What many fans around the country may not remember is that the 1977–78 Portland team was even **better** than the championship Blazers—a rare case in which hype understates reality.

The 1977–78 Blazers won 52 of their first 63 games, causing then Milwaukee coach Don Nelson to say to *Sports Illustrated*, "Those Blazers have become a team of all time." Indeed, a case could be made that those Blazers, through their first 63 games, were one of the most dominant teams ever to play in the NBA. They weren't just winning—they were blowing teams away by an average of 11.4 points per game. Only the 1971–72 Los Angeles Lakers (69–13), the 1995–96 Chicago Bulls (72–10), and the 1970–71 Milwaukee Bucks (66–16), all of whom outscored their opposition by 12.3 points per game, were more dominant in their day than Ramsay's Blazers.

In those first 63 games, the Blazers were 28–7 against teams with winning records, though they were challenged by having to play in a tough division, the Pacific, where all five teams had winning records. Moreover, 5 of their 11 losses were by 3 points or fewer. Comparing the 1977–78 juggernaut to the championship squad, Ramsay once said, "We're growing up . . . the youngest team ever to win an NBA title is a year older. Now we are more poised. We concentrate better. We have fewer dry spells on offense, fewer lapses on defense."

The Blazers made only two changes to their title-winning roster. They added 6-foot-4 rookie T. R. Dunn from Alabama, a hard-nosed defensive specialist, to replace Herm Gilliam, and then traded backup center Robin Jones to Houston for six-year veteran center Tom Owens, who proved to be invaluable in games that Walton was forced to miss. (Owens played all 82 games that season, averaging 10.1 points and 6.6 rebounds per game.) The league also reduced its rosters from 12 players to 11, so the Blazers were forced to let popular Wally Walker move on to Seattle, where, eventually, he became the Sonics' general manager.

(above) Maurice Lucas gets off a high jumper in the key against Truck Robinson and the New Orleans Jazz.
(opposite) Jack Ramsay relaxes with his players during a practice-session break.
(previous spread) Jack Ramsay with Bill Walton and Maurice Lucas, circa 1977

BEYOND THEIR ATHLETIC SKILL AND SUPERB CHEMISTRY, RAMSAY'S TEAM WAS SIMPLY THE **SMARTEST** TEAM IN BASKETBALL.

The Dunn-for-Gilliam move once again showed Stu Inman's genius. In the championship year, Portland had trouble defending big shooting guards, especially when Hollins was not in the game. Dunn proved to be the ideal stopper, strengthening the Blazer defense (in 1977–78, they gave up 4.7 fewer points per game than the championship team did).

NBA Hall of Famer Rick Barry, now a TV analyst, who often saw the Blazers play in those years, was among the many admirers of the 1977–78 club: "This team deserves any comparison anybody wants to make . . . the old Celtics, the Knicks, Philly with Wilt, L.A. with Wilt, Milwaukee with Kareem, anybody. It's a clinic whenever you play them. They get the ball and ram it down your throat. Walton is a great center who does everything, and all the rest complement each other. The Blazers may be the most ideal team ever put together."

And that team, despite its youth, had something else on its side: It knew how to prevail when the score was close, winning 10 out of 14 games that were decided by 4 points or fewer. An example of that came on January 3, 1978.

In what most Blazer fans agree is the greatest miracle finish in the history of the franchise, Portland scored 6 points in the final 13 seconds to steal a victory from the Chicago Bulls, 92–90. That's what all the post-game stories reported. Actually, though, the Blazers scored 6 points in just eight basketball seconds to overcome a 4-point deficit and seal their league-leading 29th win in 34 games.

As one *Chicago Tribune* sportswriter put it, "The jaws of defeat never lost a tooth so quickly in the history of the NBA."

Most fans, then and now, credit Lionel Hollins as the primary hero of this drama. He stole an inbounds pass and drove the length of the court to tie the game, and he was also on the finishing end of the game winner, with two seconds to spare.

But it was forward Bob Gross who set up the game winner, tipping Norm Van Lier's inbounds pass to Dave Twardzik, who threw the ball to a streaking Hollins for the game-clinching layup.

This is a game that most every Blazer fan recalls. Why? Because the highlights of it have been flashed on TV screens many times in recent years to remind basketball fans that anything is possible in the NBA. Even young Blazer fans not yet born in 1978 have probably seen it.

Yet hundreds of fans who actually attended this game never saw the miracle in person, though today they would probably deny that they left the building early. As the *Oregonian*'s Blazer beat writer Bob Robinson recalls, "With Chicago up by 4, fans were heading to the exits in droves to beat the rush out of the ice-covered Coliseum parking lot."

City streets were covered with ice following a freezing rainstorm that had hit Oregon a day earlier, bringing holiday traffic to a sliding stop. Trail Blazer president Harry Glickman had even considered calling the game off earlier in the day, but the Blazers and the Bulls couldn't find an agreeable makeup date, so they decided to play it.

To that point in NBA history, no team had ever scored so many points in so little time to win a game. The 1969–70 New York Knicks, some recalled, scored 6 points in 16 seconds to beat the Cincinnati Royals, 106–105, and stretch their winning streak to 18 games (then a record).

As the hero of the plot, Hollins, at first, seemed dazed. "It was like a storybook dream—and this dream came true," he told Robinson afterward. "I've never played on a team in high school, college, or the pros that won one like that." Lucas agreed: "I've never seen 6 points scored that quickly in

(below) Coach Ramsay relaxes during a study session.
(opposite) Bill Walton and trainer Ron Culp on the team bus
(previous spread) Coach Ramsay jumps rope as a part of his personal fitness regime.

a basketball game at any level. Lionel has remarkably quick hands. When we need a steal, he somehow gets a hand on the ball."

That the miracle of January 3, 1978, almost got postponed by the weather is a little-known irony for Blazer fans to ponder. But even more startling is that several Blazer players, including Hollins, called in before the game to say they might have trouble getting to the arena on icy streets. Trail Blazer management took no chances and dispatched four-wheel-drive transportation to pick up the players who were stranded. And just to make sure the players would get home safely after the game, the club reserved rooms at a hotel nearby.

As it turned out, the hotel rooms weren't needed. Apparently, what went on inside the building in the last 13 seconds of the game must have warmed up the whole town, because by midnight of this Cinderella story, the streets had turned to slush.

In some ways, this victory, in which Portland trailed the Bulls, 90–86, with 13 seconds remaining, was a defining moment for the defending NBA champs in a season of extraordinary basketball brilliance.

The win against the Bulls also kept alive Portland's 36-game home-court winning streak—a streak that would reach 43 before Denver beat the Blazers, 103–101, at Memorial Coliseum on February 12.

Don Nelson had always been impressed with coach Jack Ramsay's fast-breaking style of basketball, both at Philadelphia and at Buffalo, but he'd never seen it work so well, so perfectly, as it did in Portland the night of January 31, 1978. That's when Nelson had just seen his Milwaukee Bucks put together an almost perfect first half against the Blazers, scoring 39 points in the first quarter while shooting 60 percent for the half—only to find themselves trailing by 2 points by the end of the third quarter.

Portland went on to crush Milwaukee, 136–116, prompting Nelson to concede that the Blazers of that season may have been the greatest team of them all. "Ninety percent of what they do is automatic—everyone picks it up. The great Celtics teams had role-playing defensive and offensive specialists. Here, though, the attack is more general. Everybody on the Blazers can beat you at either end."

A month later, on February 28, the Philadelphia 76ers came to town in what was thought to be a sneak preview of another NBA finals matchup between the two youngest teams in the league. To this point in the 1977–78 season, Jack Ramsay's basketball team was as close to invincible as you could get in professional sports.

These Blazers were precision in motion. Portland's fast break appeared to be faster than a speeding Porsche, its frontline of Bill Walton, Maurice Lucas, Tom Owens, and Lloyd Neal more powerful than a log truck. And when a rebound was up for grabs, the Blazers seemed capable of leaping taller foes in a single bound, like Superman. The team, seemingly fueled by plasma from Krypton, was destined to take its place among the greatest basketball teams of all time. They had a chance to set an NBA record for home-court winning percentage. When they were 32–1 at home, few doubted that they would win their last eight home games and finish the season with a 40–1 record at friendly Memorial Coliseum. They were that good.

With seven players scoring in double figures and nine players scoring 8 or more points per game, the Blazers ruled the NBA just like the great Celtics teams of the 1950s and '60s had done. Beyond their athletic skill and superb chemistry, Ramsay's team was simply the smartest team in basketball. And they were showing all these attributes on the court each and every night.

Against the Sixers, the team with the second-best record in the league, the Blazers never looked better. With what Ramsay called "picture-perfect execution" (they registered 36 assists for the 41 field goals they made), Portland routed Philadelphia, 113–92, for their 50th win and the largest margin of defeat for the 76ers all season. And they did it without Mountain Man Walton, who rolled his left ankle 16 minutes into the game. Though no one realized it at the time, this was the start of the plague that destroyed the boys of winter.

So while the 50–10 record may have seemed to make Portland the team of destiny, disaster loomed as the Ides of March approached. As it turned out, the left ankle was the least of Walton's problems. Five days after he rolled it, he underwent surgery to relieve pressure on the nerves in his right foot. This pressure had caused him to put more weight on his left leg, thus causing the sprained ankle. He missed the rest of the regular season.

So depressed were the Blazers at the prospect of losing their chance at all-time greatness that Inman began to scan the globe for any healthy but unemployed basketball players. He found one in Detroit—the 6-foot-7 retired veteran Willie Norwood, who was working in a factory when he got the call from Inman on March 3. He was on the next plane to Portland. Norwood had been a physical inside banger in his four seasons at Detroit (1971–75), where Ramsay, then coaching at Philadelphia and Buffalo, had had plenty of chances to evaluate his game. In Portland's championship season, Willie played a career-high 76 games with Seattle and Ramsay again got a close and personal look at him and liked what he saw. With the Blazers, Norwood played only 19 games, even starting a couple, but the team went 7–12 in those games.

Disaster struck the Blazers again in a 128–117 loss in New York. Neal and Lucas collided in pursuit of a loose ball and Neal suffered a strained ligament in the same knee that had been operated on twice. He, too, would be sidelined for the rest of the season. And sadly, at age 28, he was to play only four more games in his NBA career. Like a contagious virus, injuries continued to attack the core of the team as Bob Gross broke an ankle March 23 in Milwaukee and was out for the year.

At this point, the best-ever Blazers resembled a hospital ward in sneakers. Game by game, injury by injury, the window was closing on what could have been the greatest team in Trail Blazer history. The wounded Blazers drew a first-round bye in the playoffs but lost, 4–2, to Seattle in the semifinals. Walton played only two games.

They had been the definition of grace in action, but their hopes for greatness in the days ahead were reduced from a shout to a whisper.

(opposite) Coach Ramsay's insistence on keeping physically fit began with the man himself. (below) Lionel Hollins awaits the beginning of yet another bus ride.

Rookie guard T. R. Dunn eats alone in a restaurant as part of the team's travel routine.

Three years after the Trail Blazers won the NBA championship, captivating thousands of Oregonians for life, the bloom had fallen off Rose City—at least temporarily. Even though the memories of the glory days of the franchise were still deeply imbedded in the minds of true Blazer fans, that championship team was gone. The dreams of a revival were still alive, but the "Red Hot & Rollin'" banners were packed away in attics and trunks like last year's holiday decorations.

That's when the late David Halberstam, a Pulitzer Prize–winning author and a literary icon, came to town to spend a year trying to find out what had happened to the team he believed could have changed the face of professional basketball.

In his book *Breaks of the Game*, about the rise and fall of the Blazers, Halberstam reveals his affection for the team and illustrates why he thought it was different from most other teams of that era. In the chapter entitled "Prologue to the Season," Halberstam explains on paper what he had told me earlier, when we both spent a week with the Trail Blazers on the road to New Jersey, Washington, Philadelphia, Boston, and Milwaukee.

"That spring, in 1977," Halberstam writes, "they had won the championship, the youngest team in history to do so, and the exuberance of their youth and the profusion and seeming perfection of their many talents, and their rare ability to control their own egos, had seemed to promise yet more, not just that something was over and accomplished, but that it had only just begun."

That the Trail Blazers' specialness had vanished in just three years was Halberstam's only disappointment in doing his research for the book—one that many reviewers today believe is the best book ever written about professional basketball.

So where did the youthful, innocent, selfless Blazers go? Halberstam speculated the last time we talked that beyond the many injuries it endured, the 1976–78 team was probably the victim of the changing times, as the NBA grew to occupy a much larger place on the national stage.

(below) Bill Walton signs autographs for fans.
(opposite) An exhausted Walton on the bench.

"I guess it was inevitable, given human nature and the allure of fame and fortune, for athletes and kids to succumb to peer pressure and choose individual achievements over the principles of team basketball," he said. "The Trail Blazers were so special that season, and the next one after that," he added, "I hoped they would change the sport, but the sport and the business that controls sports changed them."

It was the NBA championship finals in 1976–77 that made most everyone happy, especially CBS (at the time it was the highest-rated finals ever). And though the champion Trail Blazers and the 50–10 team that followed may not have changed basketball, as David Halberstam had hoped, they did change their standing in the Rose City forever.

Many Blazer fans over the years have pondered the question of what really happened to those 50–10 Blazers. What forces conspired to reverse their destiny?

The short answer: They simply broke.

The great promise of 1978 came to a resounding crash amid injuries to Walton, Gross, Neal, Twardzik, and Steele, as well as salary and contract disputes involving Hollins and Lucas—misfortunes that proved too much for even a century-best team to overcome.

Most important, the defection of Walton the following year over the issue of his medical treatment changed the future of basketball in Portland, suffocating BlazerMania just as surely as if Mt. Hood had erupted and buried the franchise in ashes.

And BlazerMania was silenced for a dozen years.

(opposite) Assistant coach Jack McKinney studies the playbook on the team bus.
(above) Hopes for a repeat championship were dashed in the final 22 games after a rash of injuries sidelined Walton, Neal, Gross, Twardzik, and Steele.

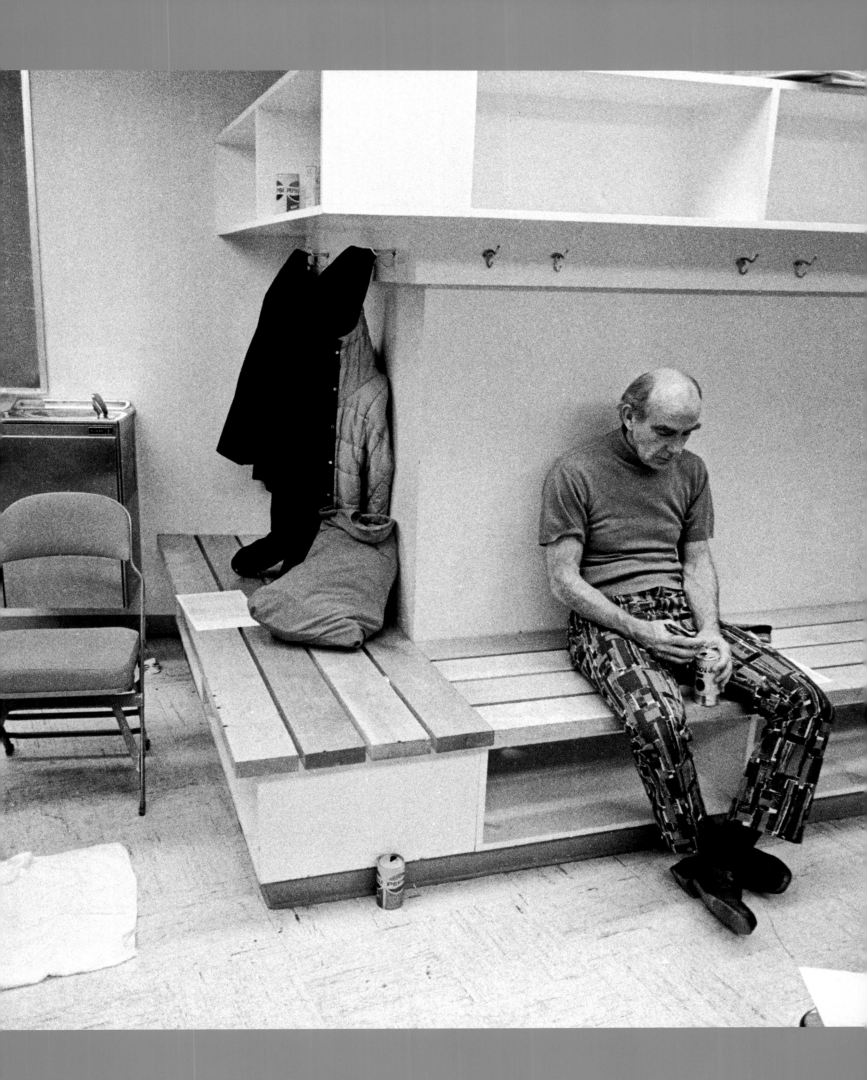

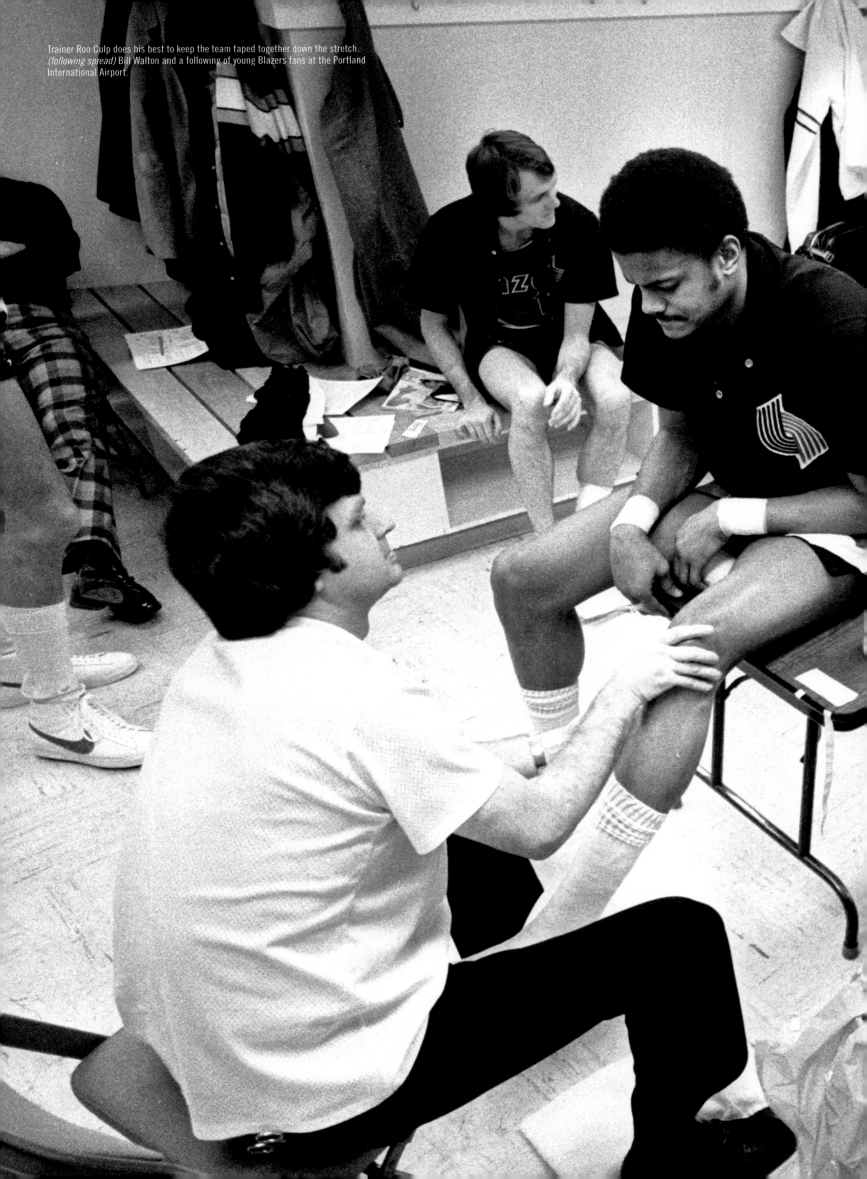

Trainer Ron Culp does his best to keep the team taped together down the stretch. *(following spread)* Bill Walton and a following of young Blazers fans at the Portland International Airport.

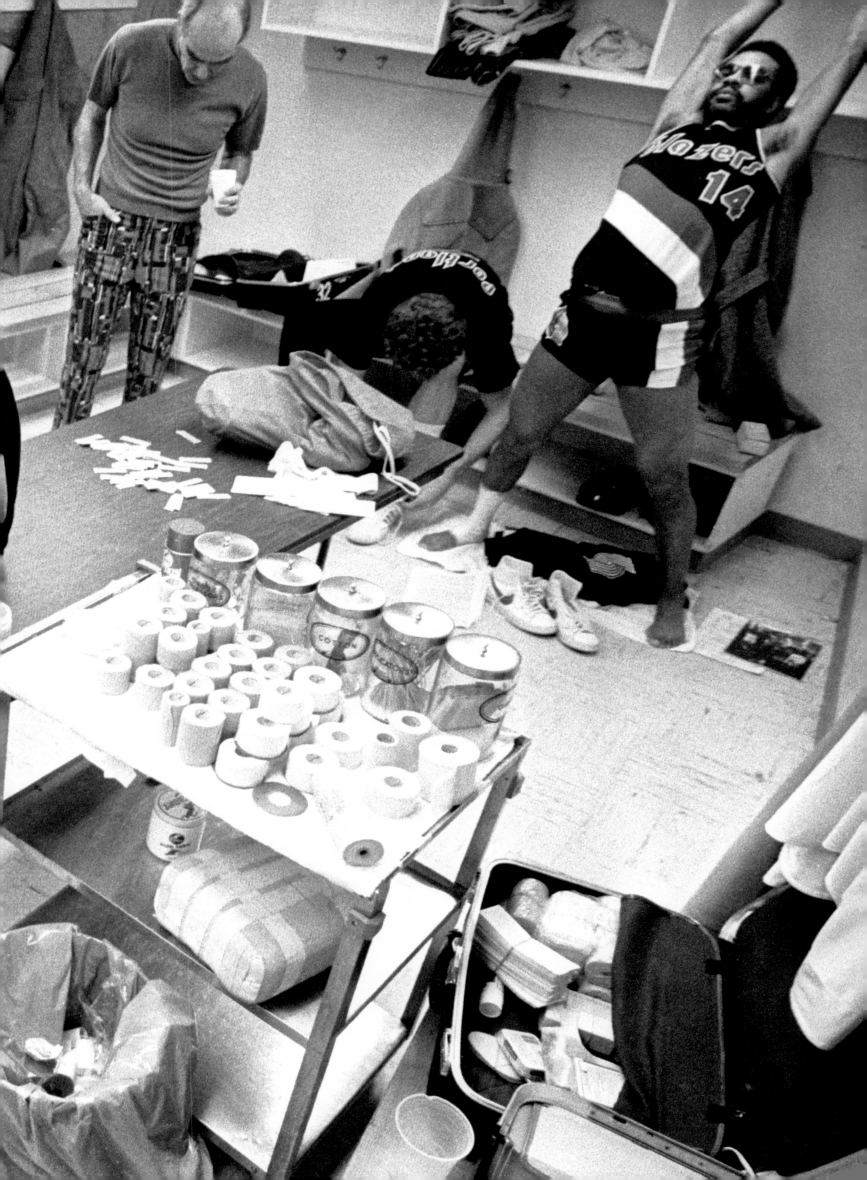

"THE TUMULT AND THE SHOUTING DIES,
THE CAPTAINS AND
THE **KINGS** DEPART"

—RUDYARD KIPLING

STRUCTION

"BLESSED ARE THE FLEXIBLE, FOR THEY SHALL NOT BE BENT OUT OF SHAPE."

—ANON.

Before passionate Trail Blazers fans could begin the long road back from their team's sudden fall from grace in late 1978, they first had to get over their devotion to the glorious past. They had to stop comparing every Trail Blazer team that followed in the 1980s with the Walton bunch. They had to learn to curb their **expectations** and just sit back and enjoy the game for what it is—exciting entertainment packed with drama, occasional humor, defining moments, and a whole bunch of what-ifs.

The NBA, most fans discovered, works on a kind of Robin Hood principle—the teams at the top are eventually doomed to fall, and the teams at the bottom, thanks to the rewards and replenishments of the NBA's college draft, are destined to rise—albeit slowly. While Portland's overnight success in going from last in its division in 1976 to NBA champion the next year was justly celebrated across America as a magnificent achievement by a wonderful team, it also had the effect of spoiling a generation of BlazerManiacs into thinking that winning titles was just a few hops, skips, and jump shots away.

That the Trail Blazers were able to beat the Robin Hood odds by making it to the playoffs for 21 consecutive years—even as they began a long and tedious rebuilding process—also had the effect of testing the patience of the average fan.

Those years leading to the Rick Adelman era—or, if you choose, the exciting and title-worthy Clyde Drexler era, circa 1984–95—were somewhat of a tease, on the cusp of greatness, but not quite there.

In between the great but short-lived dominance of the Walton years and the Rick Adelman era, some excellent players passed through Memorial Coliseum, players such as Kiki Vandeweghe, Jim Paxson, Mychal Thompson, Kermit Washington, Calvin Natt, Kelvin Ransey, Steve Johnson, Darnell Valentine, Sam Bowie, Kenny Carr, Lafayette "Fat" Lever, and Billy Ray Bates.

The 6-foot-10 forward-center Thompson and 6-foot-3 sharpshooter Ron Brewer, a pair of first-round choices that the Blazers grabbed in 1978, made fans ponder their first big what-if. What if Bill Walton hadn't left the Blazers and Thompson and Brewer had merely been additions to the 1978–79 roster, replacing Lloyd Neal and Johnny Davis? How many more world titles would that team have won?

(above) Jeff Lamp was the Blazers' top draft pick in 1981.
(opposite) Sam Bowie had the size and skill to combat the league's best big men, including the Lakers' Kareem Abdul-Jabbar.
(previous spread) Blazers Fall Camp, circa 1982

There are no right answers to those questions; in a five-man game, it isn't just a matter of making smart moves. "Every team in the league can play the what-if game and win championships in their dreams," says Blazer mastermind Stu Inman. "You have to do more than tinker with the law of averages to get there. You have to work harder at rebuilding than everybody else, you have to be smarter than everybody else, and you have to have more than your share of luck." And so, with Inman in charge, and Bucky Buckwalter advancing in the Blazer management hierarchy, the rebuilding began.

The 1979 draft brought the solid all-star shooting guard Jim Paxson, who played nine seasons in Portland and became the very first Blazer to score 10,000 points, one of only five Blazers in history to do so. Power forward Kermit Washington—one of the Blazers' all-time best rebounders and defenders, along with 7-foot center Kevin Kunnert—and a 1980 first-round draft choice, came to the team in 1979 as well, part of Portland's compensation when Bill Walton declared his own free agency and signed with San Diego. (In those days, if a player jumped ship and abandoned his team, as Walton did in the summer of 1978, the league would award the aggrieved club with compensatory draft choices.)

The club traded Maurice Lucas and two first-round draft choices to New Jersey for scrappy 6-foot-6 forward Calvin Natt, one of Inman's favorites. The rookie Natt returned Inman's admiration by averaging 20.4 points in his 25 games with the Blazers in 1980. This fooled most Blazer fans into thinking it would be a special year. Portland won its first nine games in the fall of 1979, prompting talk about contending for the championship again. But on October 28, just before a home game against Phoenix, Inman popped his head out of his smoking room at Memorial Coliseum to tell me, "Don't believe all the hype, Wayne. We're not that good. We may not even finish above .500." Inman knew his team and its potential, because the new-look, non-Walton Blazers went on to suffer their first losing season since 1975–76, finishing 38–44 and losing to Phoenix in the opening round of the playoffs.

(below) Top Blazer management, including Stu Inman, Jack Ramsay, Larry Weinberg, and Bucky Buckwalter, confer during draft day. (opposite, left and right) Billy Ray Bates.

"DON'T BELIEVE ALL THE HYPE. WE'RE NOT THAT GOOD."

—STU INMAN

Remnants of the Walton gang were pretty much all gone by the dawn of the 1980s. The Blazers traded Lionel Hollins to Philadelphia for a 1981 first-round draft choice, and Dave Twardzik and Larry Steele both retired after the 1979–80 season, leaving only Bob Gross and Tom Owens to embody the memories of the great 1977–78 season.

In an effort to rebuild, Inman did acquire one of Portland's all-time best playmakers in Kelvin Ransey of Ohio State in a swap of 1980 draft choices with Chicago (Ronnie Lester).

And while Ransey was a talented leader, capable of becoming a fan favorite, most Blazer fans had already fallen in love with 24-year-old Billy Ray Bates—a throw-back to the 19th-century South. There were lapses in his social skills, and he had difficulty functioning when faced with life's ordinary challenges, yet there were virtually no holes in his game.

Because of his off-court shortcomings, Bates played the role—and sometimes milked the role—of the underdog, the innocent young man just trying to make it in a complicated world. He learned to read in Portland at age 25, and he wrote his first check as a Trail Blazer. Yet he became one of Portland's legendary figures and the all-time leading Blazer scorer in playoffs (26.7 points per game in six playoff games). The Bates story is a book unto itself. One of the many firsts that he experienced in the big leagues happened on the day he arrived in Portland and saw snow on Mt. Hood.

"Why is there snow up there and not down here on the ground?" Bates asked Trail Blazer trainer Ron Culp on their way back to the city from the airport. After a discussion about temperature changes, weather patterns, and the fact that snow sometimes changes to rain at lower elevations, Bates just shook his head. "Snow must just have a mind of its own," he said.

In addition to the many memorable things Bates did off the court, including being the poster child for a statewide "Drink Milk" campaign in which his milk mustache decorated billboards all across Oregon, Bates is probably best remembered for one game, on December 30, 1980, and for one second, which is heralded today by Blazer fans as the most magical second in team history: Bates soars high on the baseline to take an inbounds pass from Kermit Washington. He catches the ball at waist level, spins in the air, and banks home the game-winning shot as the buzzer sounds. No dunk, just a layup that softly kills a really great Philadelphia 76ers team. And the Blazers did it on an out-of-bounds play from midcourt, with just one second on the clock.

The season's highlight reel consists of that one play. After a horrendous 7–19 start to the season, the Blazers had put together their best month in franchise history, up to that time, winning 12 of 14 games.

Beating Philadelphia in that miraculous manner put the Blazers at 13–2 for the month and back in the hunt in the Pacific Division with 20 wins, 20 losses. The surge prompted the ever-cautious Ramsay to say, "Twenty-twenty is good vision, and it should enable us to look into the future. I think we're a playoff team now. And once we get there, we could go somewhere."

This turned out to be a false prophecy. The Blazers finished with a 45–37 record, third in the division. Then they were ousted by the Kansas City Kings in the first round of the NBA playoffs, two games to one.

For Bates, whose brief NBA career seemed more like a work of fiction than fact, the heroics against the Sixers had special meaning. Philadelphia was the team that had cut him just before the 1979–80 season.

"You know, I really wanted to beat these guys," Bates said afterward. "I really wanted to play for Philadelphia, but they didn't want me." As half-court-length lob passes go, Kermit Washington's toss from midcourt wasn't that remarkable. It came to Bates low and to the right of the basket. "I could have dunked it," Bates said, "but since there was only one second left, I didn't want to chance it." Wise decision, for, in truth, his catch, 180-degree spin toward the basket, and banked layup, all in one motion, consumed the entire precious second. A dunk might have come too late.

The Sixers came into the game with a league-best 33–6 record, but having lost two games in a row, they were in no mood to crown Washington-to-Bates as the next Terry Bradshaw–to–Lynn Swann combination. Meanwhile, the celebrating Blazers piled onto Bates at midcourt after Blazer guard Kelvin Ransey tackled him.

Bates watched the Play over and over again at home that night on television. "I couldn't go to sleep," he said. "I walked in the door and turned on the television and there was the play again."

The 1980–81 season, much like the one before it, was a big tease for Blazer fans. Portland started the season with a 13–2 record and finished it by winning 12 of their

(above) Billy Ray Bates is tackled by joyous teammates after his incredible game-winning shot against Philadelphia in December of 1980.
(opposite) A relaxed 1982 pre-game courtside lineup with Steve Jones, team founder Harry Glickman, Dave Twardzik, and Bill Schonely.

final 16 games. In the middle, though, the Blazers were 20–31. Still, it was a seven-game improvement over the year before and offered a promise that young Mychal Thompson and Jim Paxson would lead the Blazers in another chorus of "Red Hot & Rollin'."

While this didn't happen, the Blazers were never really a bad team in those post-Walton years. Jack Ramsay's teams, at their very least, were always competitive. From 1979 to 1984, the Trail Blazers had only one losing season and missed making the playoffs only once (they were 42–40 in 1981–82, missing out on the playoffs in the final week of the season). Even though Thompson (20.8 points and 11.7 rebounds per game), Paxson (18.9), Natt (17.7), Ransey (16.1), and Bates (11.1) produced close to their career-best stats, the Blazers missed the playoffs by losing three of their last four games.

Put another way, in the 12 years that separated the great 1977–78 Blazers from the Clyde Drexler–led 1989–90 team that returned to the NBA championship finals, Portland's record was 487 wins and 415 losses. They had reached a median point between zenith and nadir—too good to get help from the high end of the NBA player draft, and too weak to become a contender without it. Alas, the NBA's law-of-averages formula, which supposedly lifts bottom-feeders to the top, rarely works for teams stuck in the middle. They have to swim their own way up.

If there was a glimmer of light for the Blazers in the 1980s, it was beamed to Earth by the 1982–83 squad, led by Paxson (21.7 ppg) and Natt (20.4 ppg). The team finished ninth in the NBA with a 46–36 record, including a 15-game home-court winning streak from mid-November to mid-January. Most encouraging, though, was that Portland advanced beyond the first round of the playoffs for the first time since

Clyde Drexler signs an autograph for a young fan.

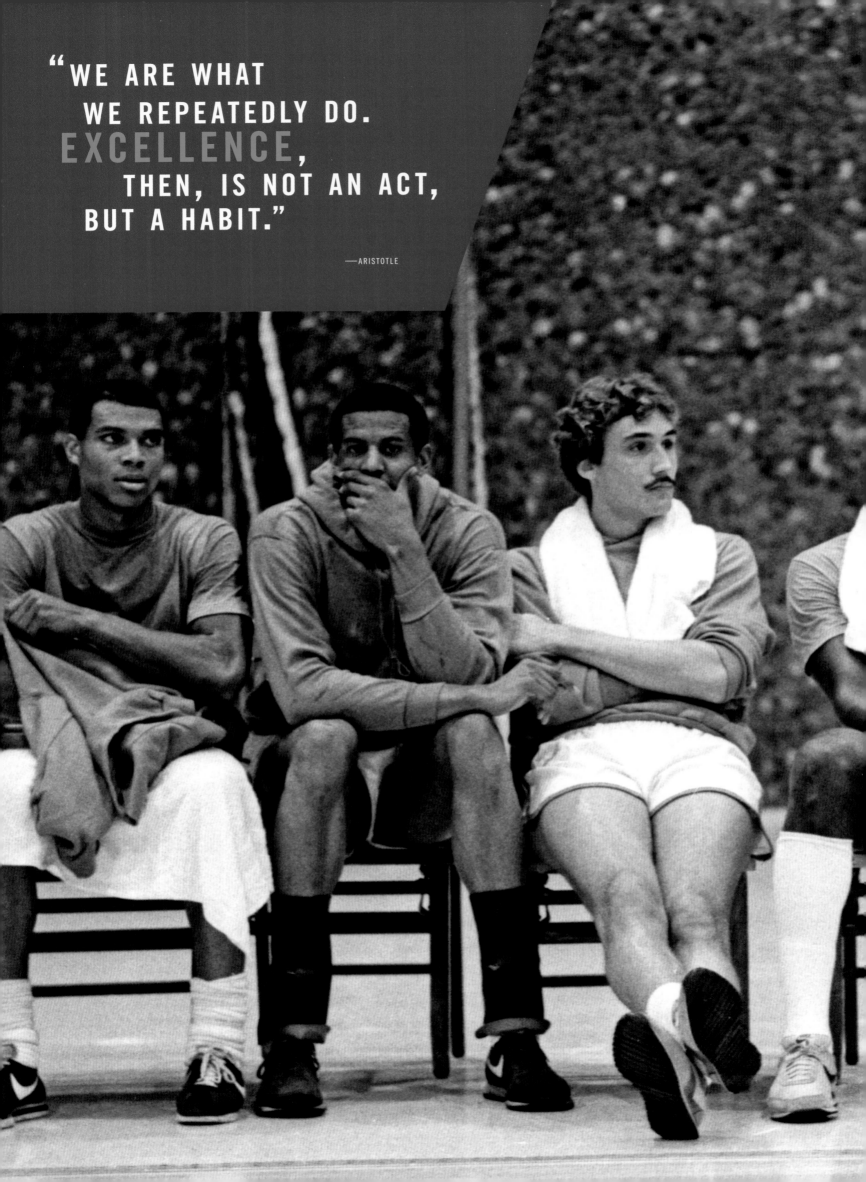

"WE ARE WHAT WE REPEATEDLY DO. EXCELLENCE, THEN, IS NOT AN ACT, BUT A HABIT."

—ARISTOTLE

1977, defeating Seattle before losing to the Lakers in the Western Conference semifinals.

Inman and Buckwalter played a major role in overhauling the roster, acquiring the solid rebounder, defender, and post-up scorer Kenny Carr in a trade with Detroit, and then trading Kelvin Ransey to Dallas for center Wayne Cooper and a 1985 first-round draft choice, who turned out to be Terry Porter. Trading the popular Ransey opened up more playing time for Darnell Valentine, who was a better defender than Ransey, with sophisticated point-guard skills. One of the keys to this team's success was a relatively injury-free run by the six core players in Jack Ramsay's rotation (Paxson, Natt, Thompson, Carr, Cooper, Valentine, and Lever). Collectively, they missed eight games all season.

The 1982–83 team earns high-fives for launching the Blazers into the playoffs for the first of 21 consecutive years—a record that not only defied the NBA's equal-opportunity formula, but to this day is also second overall to the NBA's Philadelphia/Syracuse franchise, which qualified for 22 consecutive playoffs, from 1950 to 1971.

After the breakthrough year, the Trail Blazers started building the sometimes grand teams of the 1990s. The first step in that process was drafting All-American Clyde Drexler in 1984. He was one of the University of Houston's famous Phi Slama Jama Cougars, the team that lost to North Carolina State, 54–52, in the 1983 NCAA championship finals.

Since Jack Ramsay rarely played rookies, no matter who they were, it wasn't too surprising that Drexler logged only 17.1 minutes per game in 82 games that season. Given Ramsay's skepticism toward rookies, one might wonder how many minutes Michael Jordan would have got from Ramsay had the Blazers drafted him rather than center Sam Bowie the following year.

Mychal Thompson (above) and Kiki Vandeweghe (right) were two of the major figures in Portland's rebuilding movement during the 1980s.
(previous spread) Coach Ramsay teaches (left to right) Darnell Valentine, Wayne Cooper, Jim Paxson, and Calvin Natt during a 1983 practice.

It should be noted, though, that while Drexler showed exceptional quickness and jumping ability, he proved to be an inconsistent finisher at the basket, dipsy-doodling himself out of many easy crip shots. His perimeter jumper had no arch to it, so his outside game needed work as well. He corrected both those flaws in future seasons, through hours of practice, turning himself into a very different player. Indeed, one of his pet peeves was that the media often portrayed him as a player with so much natural ability that he didn't have to work very hard at his game. Drexler saw himself as a player who had to work harder than most other athletes to compete with the best in the league, and to achieve the level of greatness necessary for a Hall of Fame career.

Even without a major contribution from Drexler (7.7 points per game), the 1983–84 team won 48 games, aided by the NBA's best home-court record (33–8). Seven players averaged double figures, or close to it, in Ramsay's fast-break attack, from Fat Lever's 9.7 points per game to Jim Paxson's team-high 21.3 points per game.

This team gave Blazer fans much joy. They were 15–1 at home in the first half of the season and didn't lose their third home game until February 12. On March 16, the highest-scoring game in Trail Blazer history kept fans on their feet well past the bedtimes of paperboys and doughnut makers as Chicago nipped Portland, 156–155, in four overtimes. It was the longest game—3 hours, 24 minutes—in Blazer history and featured a career-high 41 points by Jim Paxson. The overtimes didn't seem to faze

Sam Bowie at a press conference with Dr. Bob Cook; Bowie was a force on the boards when he was healthy, but dealing with knee and leg problems cut short a promising career.

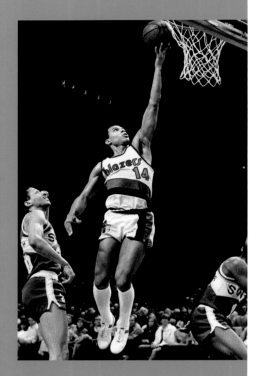

the Blazers, though, because they returned the next day to crush Golden State, 133–96.

Just when things looked the brightest—inviting BlazerManiacs of yesteryear to peek their heads out of hibernation—the team lost six of the last seven games and were ousted in the first round of the Western Conference playoffs by Phoenix.

The biggest news of the following season was the blockbuster trade that took place in the summer. That was a turning point in Trail Blazer culture as Stu Inman, Bucky Buckwalter, and Jack Ramsay agreed to turn the Trail Blazers' fortunes over to the offense. To do so, Portland traded Calvin Natt, Lafayette Lever, Wayne Cooper, and two draft choices to Denver for the league's No. 3 scorer, Kiki Vandeweghe, who averaged 29.4 points per game in 1983–84.

In his very first game with Portland, Vandeweghe scored 47 points as the Blazers trounced Kansas City, 140–119. With him as the go-to guy, the offense was overpowering, with seven players in double figures, topped by Vandeweghe's 22.4, followed by Mychal Thompson (18.4), Paxson (17.9), Drexler (17.2), Darnell Valentine (11.6), Kenny Carr (10.4), and Portland's No. 1 draft choice, Sam Bowie (10.0). Yet this turned out not to be the Blazers' year, either. Portland's win-loss record dipped to 42–40 for fifth seed in the West. As the team entered the opening-round five-game playoff series against the upstart Dallas Mavericks, hope was not an abundant commodity, even among faithful BlazerManiacs.

Indeed, it had been eight years since the Blazers had won their one and only championship, so talk on the street that spring was more about baseball and golf than about Portland's chances of advancing past the first round of the playoffs. When the Blazers closed out the Mavericks, 122–109 and 115–113, to advance to the Western Conference semifinals against the Lakers, public interest in Portland basketball picked up a little.

Then it was summer.

(above) Darnell Valentine, a popular backcourt player in the 1980s.
(below) Mike Schuler, 1987 NBA Coach of the Year, talks offensive strategy during a practice session.
(opposite) Mychal Thompson, a standout for the Blazers at both forward and center in the post-Walton years.

The 1985–86 edition proved to be another big step toward the greatness of the 1990s, as Rick Adelman, who had been coaching at Chemeketa Junior College in Salem, was hired as Ramsay's assistant, and Jerome Kersey, of little-known Longwood College in Virginia, was drafted by Inman, at Buckwalter's urging, in the second round. That summer, the Blazers added Terry Porter of Wisconsin–Stevens Point to the mix. (Portland had gained that pick when it traded Kelvin Ransey to Dallas in 1982.) So, all of a sudden, Drexler, Kersey, and Porter were on the Blazer roster, getting to know the new basketball brain on the block, Rick Adelman.

From 1985 to 1988, the Blazers were good, but not great. They also were the highest-scoring team in Portland history, averaging 115.1 points per game in 1985–86, then a franchise-high 117.9 in 1986–87, and 116.1 in 1987–88. In those three seasons, Portland's win-loss record was an outstanding 142–104, but despite the Blazers' regular-season successes, they were just 3–9 in the playoffs, eliminated without a peep in the first round every year.

(opposite) Guard Jim Paxson was the first Blazer to top the 10,000-point mark. (above) Clyde Drexler, in an early game in his 11-plus seasons in Portland, shoots against Larry Bird and the Boston Celtics.

The Vandeweghe/Drexler scoring duo, though, was fun to watch, Vandeweghe averaging 26.9 points per game and Drexler a happy 21.7. They were the best one-two punch the Blazers had had since Geoff Petrie and Sidney Wicks competed for scoring honors in the early 1970s.

Other notable happenings in the 1980s: Jack Ramsay, in 1986, left as Portland's coach after 10 successful seasons (453 wins, 367 losses, nine playoff appearances, and one NBA title), replaced by Mike Schuler, who was named NBA Coach of the Year in 1987. Bucky Buckwalter, who became vice president of basketball operations, replacing Inman after his 16 fruitful years as Portland's chief talent scout, was an active trader in 1986. He traded star center-forward Mychal Thompson to San Antonio for Steve Johnson, partly because, at this point, the Blazers were becoming worried that their 7-foot-1 center, Sam Bowie, was injury prone. They needed to get someone stronger than Thompson to play center. Bowie had played only 38 games in the 1985–86 season and, right on cue, he went down in the first exhibition game of the preseason, opening the door for Johnson to take over.

Johnson could best be described as a banger, with a wide variety of offensive weapons at his disposal around the basket. One of his best games as a Blazer came November 22, 1987—by all accounts, just another dark, damp, and dreary day in the Oregon autumn. It was cold, too. Winter, make no mistake, was dead ahead.

The Trail Blazers center was in no mood to talk about football as he drove to work that Sunday before Thanksgiving. It was the day after the annual Civil War game, in which his alma mater, Oregon State, suffered an embarrassing 44–0 loss at the hands of hated rival Oregon.

As the 6-foot-10 Johnson walked through the players' entrance at Memorial Coliseum for a late-afternoon basketball game against the Indiana Pacers, an usher said to him, "Sorry about yesterday."

Johnson frowned. "I'm taking it out on them tonight," he said as he pointed toward the visitor's dressing room. It was prophetic, to say the least. Johnson, the former OSU All-American and the Trail Blazers' Most Valuable Player the season before, had one of his finest career games as the Blazers came from behind in the second half to beat

Coach Mike Schuler with his high-scoring combo of Clyde Drexler, Kiki Vandeweghe, Kenny Carr, Terry Porter, and Steve Johnson.

Jack Ramsay's Pacers, 120–110. This was a pivotal season for the young Trail Blazers, still in the process of rebuilding their image following the gradual decline of the great Ramsay teams of the late 1970s and early '80s.

Portland was out to prove that its 1986–87 campaign, when the Blazers surprised the league with a 49–33 record, was no fluke. However, the Blazers had fallen on hard times, dropping five of their first seven games.

They needed wins. They needed to change course. They needed Steve Johnson, who was forced to play center in Bowie's absence, to step up the way he had done the season before. Johnson, after all, had had a great deal to do with Portland's surprising success in the 1986–87 campaign. He'd had his greatest season as a pro, scored in double figures 66 times, averaged 16.8 points and 7.2 rebounds per game, and finished eighth in the league in field goal percentage.

This season, though, as Thanksgiving neared, the Blazers were just 3–5. Indiana, on the other hand, was flourishing. Under their new coach, Jack Ramsay, the Pacers were on a roll, having defeated Denver and Sacramento on their short West Coast road trip. At the start of Thanksgiving week, Ramsay was looking forward to a warm homecoming of sorts in Memorial Coliseum.

However, true to his pregame boast, Johnson was keeping the Blazers in the game with, you guessed it, layups. He had 27 first-half points on 10 of 13 shooting. Possession after possession, Johnson bowled over the Indiana frontline of Steve Stipanovich, Wayman Tisdale, and Stuart Gray as though they were duckpins—Oregon Duckpins. Through three quarters, Johnson scored 34 of his game-high 36

(below) Maurice Lucas's family looks on as Harry Glickman and team owner Paul Allen congratulate Lucas on the night his number is retired.
(opposite) Former Oregon State big man Steve Johnson powers through the key for the Blazers.

points to lead the Blazers to their come-from-behind victory. Connecting on 14 of 20 floor shots for the game, Johnson became the focus of Portland's offensive strategy. He simply wore down the Pacers as the Blazers hammered the ball inside.

"I think he's the toughest post-up guy in basketball, other than perhaps Kevin McHale," Ramsay said after the game.

Schuler also took note of Johnson's performance, which included 12 rebounds in 38 minutes, with only 3 personal fouls—this from a player who'd led the NBA the season before in disqualifications.

"Steve was magnificent," Schuler praised. "He really took it to them. They refused to double team him in the first half, so he simply made them pay." The victory over Indiana was the start of a big turnaround for the Blazers. They went on to win their next seven games en route to a 53-win season, the second best in Trail Blazer history, up to then.

The season proved, however, to be a mix of joy and frustration for Johnson. He was named to the All-Star team for the first time, largely on his early-season play, but injuries to his ankle, knee, and thumb forced him to miss 39 games, including the All-Star game.

For a guy who had just turned 30 earlier in the month, this was going to be the start of something grand. Instead, it was his last great game as a Blazer.

For Buckwalter, the summer of 1986 was his watershed moment as a Blazer personnel director. After trading Mychal Thompson for Johnson in early June, he drafted the athletic but ignoble Walter Berry, then traded Berry after seven games to San Antonio for 7-foot Kevin Duckworth. Bucky also became the first NBA personnel director to tap the European market for two of its greatest stars—Arvydas Sabonis of Lithuania and Drazen Petrovic of Croatia—selected in the first and third rounds of the 1986 NBA college draft. Petrovic and Duckworth became vital additions when the team reached the NBA championship finals in 1990.

In the late 1970s and early '80s, European basketball was on the rise, but few coaches, managers, or NBA league officials knew much about it. Most were skeptical, pointing out that the Euro players they'd seen were soft on defense and lacked the quickness and court creativity of American players. To some extent this was true. "But the Euro critics forgot an important difference. European players were often better fundamentally, better distance shooters, better passers, and better in understanding that basketball, after all, is a five-man, not a one-on-one, game," Buckwalter points out. In 1976, Bucky helped develop the Brazilian National Team, where he spotted and encouraged a promising 15-year-old named Oscar Schmidt, one of basketball's greatest scorers. Moreover, Bucky had excellent sources coaching teams in Europe; they'd call him every summer to tell him about their latest discovery. Having coached in college (University of Utah and Seattle University), the ABA (Utah Stars), and the NBA (Seattle Sonics), Buckwalter knew how good Sabonis and Petrovic would be in the NBA even before they knew it.

Except for the continued all-star performance of Drexler, who averaged a franchise-high 27.2 points per game, the 1988–89 season proved to be a bust and, moreover, a time of great change. Gone through trades were Paxson in 1988 and Vandeweghe in 1989. Those trades were motivated by the club's desire to rebuild around Drexler as the franchise player and to encourage the development of young Jerome Kersey, especially since the aging Vandeweghe had missed 44 games due to injury the year before and was beginning to look fragile because of a bad back.

By the spring of 1988, Paul Allen, cofounder of Seattle's software giant, Microsoft, and one of the 20 richest men in America, bought the Trail Blazers from Larry Weinberg. One of his first moves was to fire Coach Schuler and appoint Rick Adelman as interim coach. In Schuler's two and a half seasons at the Blazer helm, his record was 127–84, but several Blazer players, including Drexler, weren't happy with his coaching style. That, and the fact that he couldn't get the team out of the first round of the playoffs, proved to be his downfall.

With Allen as an aggressive owner, and one who had deeper pockets than any other owner in professional sports, a new era of Blazer basketball was launched—one that suggested that Rome, with the right leadership, really could have been built in a day or two.

(opposite) Bill Walton's number is retired on November 3, 1989, at the opening game of the team's 20th anniversary season. *(below)* New owner Paul Allen and his predecessor Larry Weinberg pose after a May 31, 1988 press conference announcing the team's sale.

DREXLER

BY WAYNE THOMPSON

Among the thousands of personnel decisions that the Trail Blazers have made in their first 40 years in the NBA, the one that will perhaps haunt them forever took place in the late spring of 1984. That's when Portland passed on North Carolina junior Michael Jordan to select 7-foot-1 Sam Bowie of Kentucky with the second pick in the NBA draft.

Naysayers still chide the Blazers for not having the clairvoyance in 1984 to predict that the young Mr. Jordan was going to become one of the greatest players in the history of the game. But who knew in 1984 that the 21-year-old Jordan, who averaged only 17.7 points per game as a collegian, would average 30.1 points a game in 15 NBA seasons? Some did, of course. Pulitzer Prize–winning author David Halberstam, for instance, once wrote, "The only person on Earth who could defend Michael Jordan was his coach, Dean Smith of North Carolina."

In his book *Playing for Keeps: Michael Jordan and the World He Made*, Halberstam says that Coach Smith, in advocating his team concept, in which no single player was greater than the whole, never allowed Jordan to become the Tar Heels' go-to guy, thus Jordan's scoring production out of college seemed just ordinary.

To others, though, Jordan simply had no peers in terms of talent, and they excuse his mediocre North Carolina stats by saying that most of the players out of Smith's basketball factory (Walter Davis, James Worthy, Sam Perkins, and Phil Ford come

to mind) had deceivingly unimpressive scoring numbers.

So before the 1984 draft, you had two schools of thought among basketball people: (1) Michael Jordan was much greater than his career at North Carolina revealed, and (2) Michael Jordan was a very good basketball player, but because he played at North Carolina, there was no way to tell how good he was.

For the Trail Blazers, it really never came down to taking sides in that argument. If you follow conventional basketball wisdom, the Trail Blazers needed a center in 1984 in the worst way, and Sam Bowie, according to the majority of NBA scouts, was a center in the best way. Bowie's future at age 21 looked so bright that Jerry Krause, Chicago's vice president of basketball operations in 1984, confided once that if Portland had passed on both Jordan and Bowie, the Bulls also would have passed on Jordan and taken Bowie. Moreover, Rod Thorn, then the general manager of the Chicago Bulls, revealed years later that the Bulls were not above contemplating a trade for Jordan, and it was only when these initiatives did not pan out that they picked and kept Jordan.

What the Blazers didn't need in the 1984 college draft was a 6-foot-6 shooting guard. They already had two great scorers at that position, the veteran 6-foot-5 All-Star Jim Paxson and the budding 6-foot-7 All-Star Clyde Drexler.

So while the question about Michael Jordan's talent has been answered—he is arguably the greatest basketball player ever to lace up a pair of sneakers—it has also become obvious over the span of their careers that he and Clyde Drexler had something special in common:

Themselves.

Roll the clock back to November 29, 1991, for a game between the defending NBA champion Chicago Bulls and the upstart Blazers at Memorial Coliseum. Chicago won that game in overtime, 116–114, but Jordan, with 40 points, and Drexler, with 38, put on an offensive show that made the highlight reel on sports shows across America.

After the game, an exhausted Jordan, staring down at a stats sheet, noticed Drexler's line: 15 of 27 from the floor, 12 rebounds, 8 assists, 5 steals, 38 points.

"Sometimes, when I look at myself in the mirror, I see Clyde Drexler," Jordan said.

VS JORDAN

Coming from Jordan, it was the ultimate compliment, that Drexler was the one player in the NBA who could keep pace with him.

And while Drexler never really claimed to want to be like Mike, he was, on the basketball court, very much like Mike.

And if the 20-20-hindsight visionaries need evidence to show that Portland made the right decision in not adding Jordan to a roster that included Paxson and Drexler, they need to look no further than Portland's 137–121 victory at San Antonio on February 24, 1985.

In this game, the Blazers had to rely on their shooting guards, Paxson and Drexler, the same two players who effectively blocked Blazer management from considering taking Michael Jordan in the June 1984 NBA draft.

The Drexler-Paxson combination was good for 72 points against the Spurs. Their joint stats line: 30 of 49 floor shooting, 12 of 13 from the free throw line, 18 rebounds, 13 assists, 4 blocked shots, 5 steals, 5 personal fouls (all by Drexler), and 3 turnovers (all by Paxson).

One of the reasons why San Antonio didn't succeed in its strategy to overwhelm the Blazers on the boards was Sam Bowie—the same Sam Bowie who had kept Michael Jordan from becoming a Trail Blazer.

Bowie did a masterful job against the All-Star Artis Gilmore,

holding him to 16 points and just 10 rebounds, and much of Gilmore's production came when Bowie was on the bench.

"Sam was a catalyst in there for us," Blazers coach Jack Ramsay said. "When he gets a rebound, he gets it out of the congestion area very fast. He's a good ball handler and good passer, with the court vision usually reserved for point guards."

That's no accident. Bowie is the son of a former Harlem Globetrotter. Growing up, Sam practiced ball handling more than any other skill, and he played guard facing the basket as a youngster, before an enormous growth spurt in high school turned him into a pivot man.

In this game, Bowie's outlet passes to streaking Blazers—Drexler, Jerome Kersey (12 points), and Steve Colter (18 points)—gave Portland a decided fast-break advantage against the slower Spurs.

Now, it seems that it is Clyde Drexler, more than Bowie or Paxson, who presents the most logical justification for why the Blazers passed on Michael Jordan in the 1984 draft.

Reliving that decision decades later invites interesting speculation, since both players have been enshrined in the Naismith Memorial Basketball Hall of Fame. But answer this question:

Whose career would have suffered the most had Jordan and Drexler shared the shooting-guard minutes for the Trail Blazers?

The three-point contestants at the 1987 All-Star Game in Seattle: Boston's Larry Bird; future-Trail Blazer and then-Dallas Maverick Detlef Schrempf; Seattle's Dale Ellis; future-Trail Blazer and then-Boston Celtic Danny Ainge; Milwaukee's Sidney Moncrief; Los Angeles Lakers' Byron Scott; Los Angeles Lakers' Michael Cooper; and Portland's Kiki Vandeweghe

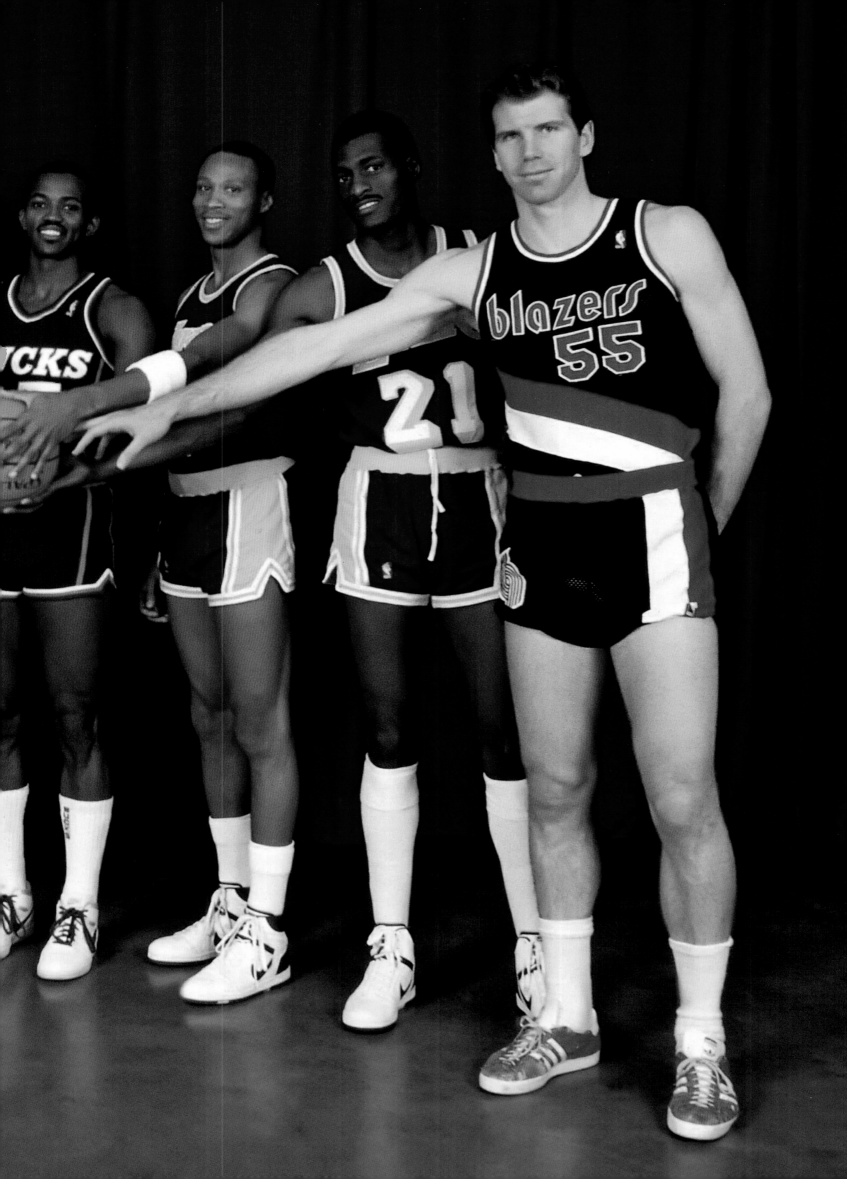

Harry Glickman and Stu Inman regularly watched Trail Blazer games from the crow's nest at Memorial Coliseum.

THE ROARING '90s

"THEY ARE ABLE BECAUSE THEY THINK THEY ARE ABLE. THEY CAN BECAUSE THEY **THINK** THEY CAN."

—VIRGIL: *THE AENEID*

The Trail Blazers teams of 1989–92 left a legacy of winning basketball, much admired throughout the sports world, but especially in **Oregon**, where national recognition for excellence in any field is worth celebrating.

Team chemistry made the Blazers exceed all rational expectations—and so quickly, too—as well as their unabashed confidence and swagger. As the Roman poet Virgil suggested more than 2,000 years ago (and I apologize for paraphrasing), "You can be a winner if you see yourself as a winner." To a man, the Blazers of 1989–90 thought they were worthy, so they were worthy. Even when the odds were stacked against them, the Blazers seemed to will themselves to victory.

An example of this inner strength came four days before Christmas in 1989. Looking back on Portland's surprising journey to the 1990 NBA championship finals, there were a few hints early on that the Blazers had the moxie to make the trip. One was a Friday-night shootout at Dallas against the high-scoring Mavericks. The road-weary Blazers, who had lost three straight games, weren't creating much of a stir in the Pacific Division. Dallas, on the other hand, had won four straight and were beginning to look like contenders in the Midwest.

Losing 8 of 13 road games, the Blazers, when out of town, seemed a different team from the one with the sparkling 13–2 mark at home. At this stage, they simply were trying to discover better living through chemistry in Rick Adelman's first full season as head coach.

And on this chilly December night in Dallas, Portland just might have found it, storming back from a 14-point third-quarter deficit to tie the game in regulation and then outlast the Mavs in triple overtime, 144–140.

It was a victory, Adelman said afterward, that could last a long time. "This type of game is a momentum builder and a season maker. To hang in there and win this game—well, the guys were just mentally so tough, they just refused to lose."

Tired, with injuries to key bench players (Mark Bryant, Byron Irvin), and trailing for most of the game, the Blazers not only stormed back to tie the game in the fourth quarter, but also overcame a 5-point Dallas lead with two minutes left in the second overtime to force a third extra period.

Portland eventually won the marathon because it outshot Dallas from the field and the foul line and turned the ball over only 12 times in 63 minutes of playing time. With the score tied at 138-all in the final overtime, Kevin Duckworth, the unlikely hero, canned a short jumper with a minute to go, giving the Blazers a lead they never relinquished.

(above) Rick Adelman
(opposite) In an amazing show of support, thousands of BlazerManiacs rally at Pioneer Courthouse Square after Portland lost 4–1 to the Detroit Pistons in the 1990 NBA Finals.
(previous spread) The Blazers were a big draw on the road during the '90s.

Dallas guard Rolando Blackman, a Blazer killer through most of his career, missed a jump shot. Moments later, Terry Porter, who turned in a magnificent performance with 28 points, 10 assists, 6 rebounds, and 5 steals in 52 minutes, drove the lane, scored, was fouled, and connected on the free throw to give Portland an insurmountable 143–138 lead.

Clyde Drexler's offensive line came close to cloning that of Porter. In 55 minutes, Drexler had 32 points, 8 assists, and 9 rebounds, just missing out on the 16th triple double of his career. But he also probably made the most important field goal of this season with 21.1 seconds left in regulation when he tied the game with a 3-point field goal from the corner—the only 3-pointer the Blazers got in this game.

The Blazers, including Adelman, seemed drained by the 3-hour, 10-minute marathon, but Drexler claimed he never got tired, even though he played every minute of the game after halftime.

"This was a great game—one of the best I've ever played in," Drexler said afterward. "It reminded me of some of those playoff games here in 1985," when the Blazers eliminated Dallas in the first round of the NBA playoffs, three games to one.

Both coaches, not looking for moral victories, were reluctant to substitute any players in the overtime. But veteran Wayne Cooper and rookie Cliff Robinson proved to be able replacements, Cooper adding 11 points and 8 rebounds to the cause and Robinson, in a robust 40 minutes of action, collecting 14 points and 8 rebounds. "It was an unbelievable game," said a tired Cooper. "It was just one of the best I've ever played in—a great way to end 1989 and the decade."

Dallas coach Richie Adubato was willing to give the game ball to Drexler for his clutch 3-point bomb from the corner that sent the game into overtime. "Clyde made an unbelievable shot from the corner," he said.

The victory over Dallas was, as Cooper said, a great way to end the 1980s—not a kind decade for Blazer fans who still remembered the great 1977 championship, the exciting season that followed, then the untimely breakup of the Bill Walton–led champs.

(above) Clyde "The Glide" Drexler
(below) Byron Irvin, Drazen Petrovic, Clifford Robinson, and Nate Johnston erupt off the bench after a key play during the 1990 playoffs.

With all the optimism of a New Year's resolution, many fans hoped that the 1990s would revive BlazerMania. And the '90s did. After that three-overtime shootout in Dallas, the Blazers went on to post a 44–13 record the rest of the season, finishing with a then franchise-best 59 wins.

Adelman's troops rode what he called "this season-maker" victory at Dallas all the way to the Western Conference championship and a shot at the world-champion Detroit Pistons.

It was the start of a run that lasted five seasons—a run in which the Blazers averaged 55 wins a year and did bring BlazerMania back to life.

In that regard, the team reflected the spirit and character of their new coach, whose approach to every challenge was also Virgilian: "Anything is possible if you believe it is possible," he preached. The Blazers became the most explosive team ever, leading the league in many aspects of the game—rebounding, 3-point shooting, running the fast break, selflessness, and above-the-rim athleticism.

(above) Portland Trail Blazers owner Paul Allen

Led by Hall of Fame superstar Clyde Drexler, the early-'90s Blazers averaged almost 60 wins a season, reaching the NBA Finals twice (in 1990 and '92). If not for their misfortune of peaking at the same time that the Chicago Bulls were starting their reign, the Blazers no doubt would have achieved dynastic status.

In those three seasons (1989–92), the Blazers won 179 games, just 4 games fewer than Michael Jordan's Bulls. Yet nobody expected sudden greatness from this team. Coming off a disappointing 39–43 record the year before (1988–89), the Blazers caught fire in March and April, finishing the regular season by winning 21 of their last 26 games. But perhaps the real key to the Blazers' spring was that they finally learned how to succeed on the road as never before, winning 11 of their last 14 road games. Entering the playoffs, the 1989–90 Blazers set then all-time team records for wins (59), road wins (24), and team confidence, as they fashioned the second-best record in the NBA. Many would call this Clyde Drexler's team, but, truth be told, the key to this turnaround was an off-season trade that sent center Sam Bowie and a draft choice to New Jersey for Charles Linwood "Buck" Williams. In addition, Drazen Petrovic got more playing time down the stretch and added firepower off the bench, and rookie Cliff Robinson emerged as one of the best on-the-ball defenders ever to play for the Blazers.

Williams was a banger, a defensive stopper, an intimidator, and clearly the key to the great Trail Blazer teams that dominated most NBA opponents from 1989 through 1993. He was the defensive anchor of those glory teams of the early '90s, doing the dirty work on a team that needed stoppers. Without Buck, there would have been no 59 wins, no playoff finals. The deal also helped Stu Inman's legacy because trading Bowie for Williams set aside the 1984 draft debate over Sam Bowie versus Michael Jordan for future generations to decide.

Portland breezed through the opening round of the playoffs, sweeping Dallas, 3–0. But then they struggled somewhat against San Antonio, finally winning the seven-game series by downing the Spurs in two dramatic overtime victories at home.

Next came the Western Conference finals against Phoenix, a team that had beaten the Blazers twice in the regular season and had crushed them in the first two playoff games in the Valley of the Sun by the lopsided scores of 123–89 and 119–107. By winning three games at friendly Memorial Coliseum by the narrowest of margins (100–98, 108–107, and 120–114), the Blazers earned the right to face the Suns May 31 in Game 6 at Phoenix.

Coach Rick Adelman sets the strategy during a time out.

Clinging to a 3–2 lead in a series in which the Suns had outscored them 561 points to 424, the Blazers willed themselves to the Western Conference Championship by beating the Suns, 112–109, at Veterans' Memorial Coliseum in Phoenix. In the end, few would disagree that the blue-collar Blazers, who scored the final 6 points of this game with clutch defensive stops, deserved a berth in the NBA Finals.

All the Blazer starters had great games to set the Suns. Besides Williams, who had 12 points and 11 rebounds, and Kersey, who added 15 points and 10 rebounds, Drexler collected 23 points, 11 rebounds, and 7 assists; Porter added 23 points and 7 assists; and Kevin Duckworth contributed 18 points and 8 rebounds. But it was the rookie guard Drazen Petrovic, perhaps the greatest outside shooter the Blazers have ever had, who set the tone at the start of the fourth quarter as he scored 7 straight points, including a 3-point bomb, to turn an 89–84 deficit into a 91–90 Blazer lead with 10 minutes left.

It was a special moment for the late, great Croatian. About to become the first European basketball player to make it to the NBA championship series, Drazen had relished his role in the Phoenix win (5 for 7 shooting and 11 points in nine minutes of playing time). Once back in Portland, Petrovic called his parents, his brother, and his girlfriend in Yugoslavia and then stayed up all night answering a dozen long-distance telephone calls from reporters in Europe.

Petrovic wasn't alone in marking the moment: The Blazer postgame celebration, which began in the chaos of their Phoenix dressing room, reached a height of 35,000 feet on Blazer One on the flight back to Oregon. The team landed in Hillsboro, where more than 10,000 Blazer fans gathered in the wee morning hours to cheer their heroes. There were many memorable moments in Portland's ride to the Western Conference championship in 1990, but perhaps the most vivid one was when Terry Porter came out of nowhere during the chaotic locker room celebration and jumped on Buck Williams's back, shouting, "Giddyup, Buck."

Once he dismounted, Porter explained, "When Buck came here, he said he'd carry us into the NBA Finals. I just wanted to see what a real ride on his back would be like."

After escaping Phoenix, with the Western Conference championship in hand, the Blazers were heavy underdogs in the NBA Finals, just as they had been 13 years and two days earlier when they faced the Philadelphia 76ers in 1977. And yet here they were, defying the odds once again by beating the Bad Boys, a.k.a. the Detroit Pistons, on the road in the second game of the 1990 NBA Finals. Here, once again, was a fledgling Blazer team that wasn't supposed to contend for a title this soon, and once again they shocked the pundits, mostly because, in true Virgilian fashion, they thought they could succeed.

It was Clyde Drexler's two free throws with 2.1 seconds remaining that clinched a 106–105 Portland victory to tie the series at a game apiece and brought Portland a short-lived home court advantage. The Pistons, however, swept all three games at Memorial Coliseum to recapture the title.

Nevertheless, the groundwork had been laid; the Blazers got a whiff of champagne and a taste of the glory that had been absent for the past 13 years. At the postseason party, Adelman summed up the team's mood about the season by saying, "I think we proved this year that we are as good as we think we are."

Great teams don't just happen overnight. They are put together painstakingly over many years. The Blazers of the early '90s were built primarily through the draft. Just as Stu Inman is thought to be primarily responsible for building Portland's only championship team (1976–77) and the greatest Blazer team of them all (1977–78), much of the credit for constructing the 1990s Blazers should go to Morris "Bucky" Buckwalter.

If NBA scouts received trophies for good hunting, then Bucky Buckwalter would have 10 on his mantel inscribed with these names: Clyde Drexler, Johnny Davis, Jerome Kersey, Terry Porter, Arvydas Sabonis, Drazen Petrovic, Cliff Robinson, Kevin Duckworth, Buck Williams, and Moses Malone.

(right) Terry Porter greets fans at Hillsboro Airport on May 29, 1992 after clinching a berth in the NBA Finals.

Clyde Drexler, Detroit's Bill Laimbeer, and Buck Williams battle under the rim in a 1990 NBA Finals game.

Buckwalter scouted basketball talent for the Blazers for 20 years. Over that time, he played a major role in team building, finding players that others had overlooked, and recommending players the Blazers should acquire through the draft or via trades. His philosophy is as down-to-earth as his personality. "Basketball is a game of quickness and reaction," he often said. "You have to be a good athlete, be willing to compete, and be unselfish. So you start assessing people based on their talent, athleticism, physical attributes, and temperament. But then there are the intangibles—competitiveness, desire, confidence, will to win. The great players have all that."

Buckwalter's approach to evaluating talent was different from Inman's. They both paid attention to a player's talent and basketball IQ, but the difference for Bucky was often a player's quickness, speed, and athleticism, while Inman placed more value on a player's character. Inman had uncommon perceptions about people and what made them tick. When talking about a player, one of his favorite descriptions went something like this: "I don't know if John Doe has really discovered who he is, but I think I have an idea of who he can be." Then Inman would inevitably make comparisons. About Clyde Drexler, for example, Inman once said, "He's Dominique Wilkins without the ego." About Terry Porter, he exclaimed, "He and John Stockton are a lot alike, except Terry has more range, and Stockton is a better playmaker." To describe the hustling tendencies of Darnell Valentine, Inman once said, "He has a beautiful relationship with a loose ball."

It was Buckwalter, though, who was the chief architect of the fast-breaking, athletic Portland teams that advanced to the NBA Finals in 1990 and 1992. He acquired obscure college players Terry Porter and Jerome Kersey with late draft picks, then pulled off the trade for Buck Williams that transformed the Blazers into an instant contender in 1989–90.

(top) Terry Porter cools off after scoring 26 points in 109–105 overtime win over the Lakers in Los Angeles on March 29, 1991.
(above) Terry Porter leads the charge out of the locker room.
(opposite) Bill Schonely interviews Kevin Duckworth at Memorial Coliseum's center court.

Clyde Drexler (left) and Michael Jordan (right) get ready to square off in the 1992 NBA Finals.

Named the NBA's Executive of the Year by the *Sporting News* in 1991, Buckwalter was a pioneer in bringing European players to the NBA, drafting the very best that European basketball could offer in Aryvdas Sabonis and Drazen Petrovic in 1986.

He and Inman didn't always agree. He had to persuade Inman to take Drexler with the 14th pick in the 1983 NBA college draft, based on Drexler's great leaping ability and overall athleticism. Inman was concerned about his fundamentals. What helped seal the deal, though, was Drexler's score on a psychological test administered by Inman's longtime friend Dr. Bruce Ogilvie, a clinical psychologist from San Jose State. Ogilvie had been testing athletes from the NBA and the NFL for several years in a unique evaluation of their character and personal attributes. The test measures the player's mental toughness, their will to win, and their ability to subordinate individuality for the good of the team.

After testing Drexler, Ogilvie asked Inman, "Stu, is there any way that Clyde could have seen a copy of the test?"

"Why do you ask?" Inman responded.

"Because among the thousands I've tested, only Roger Staubach of the Dallas Cowboys had a better score."

Buckwalter and Inman also disagreed in 1984 on when to take unranked Jerome Kersey in the draft. Both had scouted Kersey and liked him, but Buckwalter worried that too many other NBA scouts were at Portsmouth, Virginia, that spring, when Kersey had had a breakout tournament. Someone else was sure to see Kersey's potential. The Blazers had two first-round draft choices and four seconds that year, and time was running out on their final pick of the second round— No. 46 overall. Inman insisted that the Blazers could get Kersey in a later round, but Buckwalter felt that Kersey wouldn't be there later. General manager Harry Glickman recalls that when the phone call came in from the New York draft center to tell the Blazers they had less than a minute to make a selection, Inman shouted across the room, "Okay, Bucky, you can have Kersey, but I'm winning the next round."

A lot of Portland's success in the early 1990s had to do with team chemistry. In the summer of 1991, after his rookie season, Alaa Abdelnaby, a Duke alum, shared those thoughts with Kerry Eggers, who was then the Blazers' beat reporter for the *Oregonian*. "We all get along so well," he said. "You have a wide diversity of age and personality, but we all related to each other, all liked each other. You could go out on a given night on the road with any different combination of guys. We'd beat on each other at practice, but loved each other the rest of the time." Beyond the trophies and the triumphs, the Blazers of 1989–92 were noted for their exceptional character and strong friendships, which were uncommon in the culture of a professional sports franchise. They set a high standard of conduct and performance, a benchmark for future Trail Blazer teams to follow.

(top) Jack Nicholson look-a-like cheers on the Blazers.
(above) Terry Porter faces the pressure from Utah fans in Game 3 of the Western Conference Semifinals.
(opposite) Terry Porter poses for the cameras at the 1991 NBA All-Star Game in Charlotte, North Carolina.

A Dickensian hint of how good the 1990–91 season was to be came November 25, 1990: It was the best of times for the Portland Trail Blazers and perhaps the worst of times for the San Antonio Spurs. It was a night of very magical happenings.

Off to their best start in franchise history, the Blazers annihilated a very talented San Antonio team, 49–18, in a first quarter fit for a time capsule. The first-quarter play-by-play pages read like bad fiction. Where's the gritty reality? Where's the drama? Who would believe it? Portland connected on 22 of its 25 floor shots, including all five of its 3-point bombs, and doled out a club-record 18 assists.

Oh, yeah—Jerome Kersey missed a free throw.

The Spurs, the same team that gave the Blazers fits in the Western Conference semifinals six months earlier, were stunned. David Robinson summed up San Antonio's reaction best: "That's the best first quarter I've ever seen. I mean, come on. Have you seen a better first quarter than that? That was phenomenal." This was truly one for the record books: the quintessential quarter of basketball at any level. The Trail Blazers

"THEY WERE AS GOOD IN THAT FIRST 12 MINUTES AS ANY TEAM I'VE EVER SEEN PLAY THIS GAME."

—LARRY BROWN

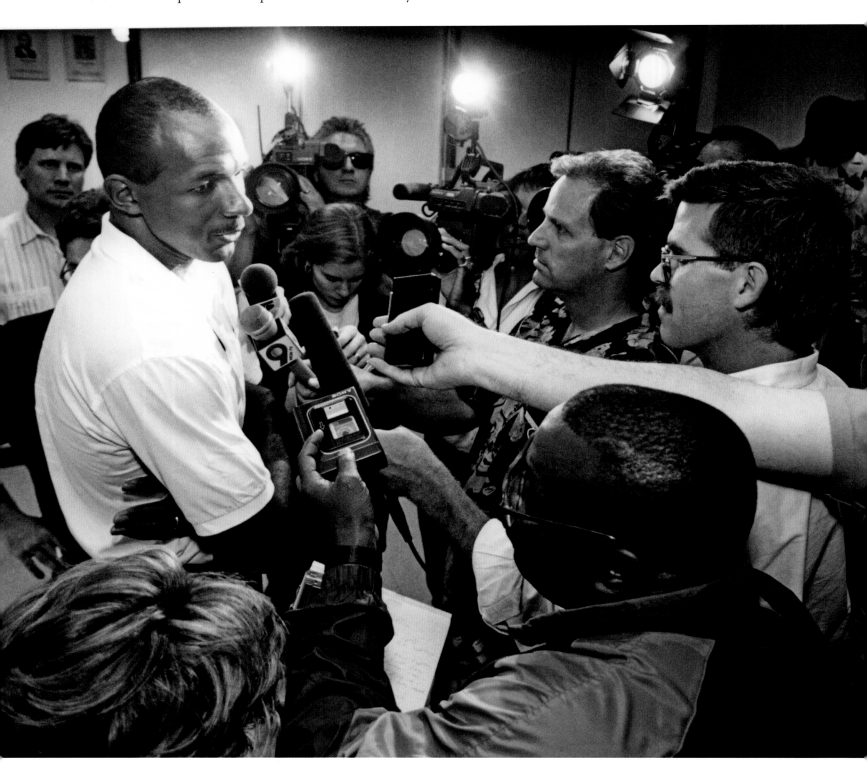

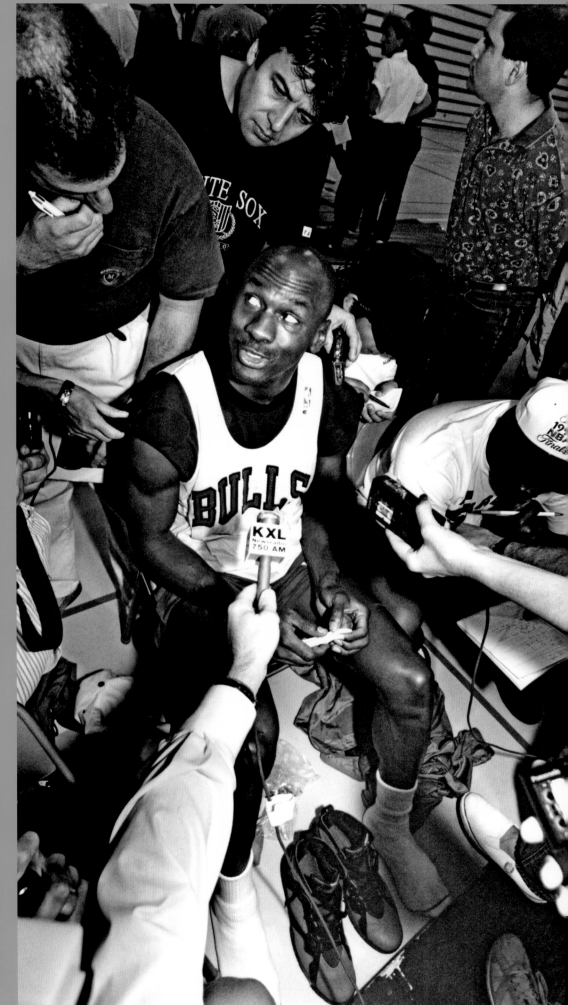

Clyde Drexler *(below)* and Michael Jordan *(right)* were the star media attractions during the 1992 NBA Finals.

played what was arguably the best 12 minutes of basketball in NBA history.

This wasn't garbage time against an inferior opponent. San Antonio entered the game with a 7–2 record; the Blazers were 10–0. This was the first taste of serious combat in the 1990–91 season between two NBA championship contenders.

San Antonio coach Larry Brown made no excuses and, surprisingly, hardly found fault with the way his team played in that quarter.

"Perhaps they [the Blazers] were a little more into the game at the start than we were, but still . . . they were terrific. Their bench was terrific. They would have beaten the All-Decade team tonight. They were as good in that first 12 minutes as any team I've ever seen play this game."

The Blazers hit their first 7 shots, scored the first 6 points of the game, then led by scores of 16–3, 28–9, and 46–18 before getting a long 3-pointer from Cliff Robinson with 6 seconds left in the quarter.

Clyde Drexler never played better. He connected on 7 of 8 floor shots, including a long 3-pointer, had 3 of Portland's 8 rebounds, 4 assists, 2 steals, and 4 blocked shots: 15 points. Blazer center Kevin Duckworth was 6 for 6 from the floor, as the Spurs seemed content to allow him to shoot his unique jumper, delivered shot-put-style.

Terry Porter set a Blazers record (at the time) with 10 assists in the quarter, 4 of them to set up Duckworth's jumpers. Porter also made all 3 of his field-goal attempts, including two 3-pointers.

So, who missed shots for Portland? Kersey, who went 2 for 3 in the quarter, missed the first one. Buck Williams, after hitting his first 2 field goal tries, missed the second one. And Drexler, probably due to fatigue, missed the third one. That was it.

Having made it to the NBA Finals in 1990 and starting the season at 10–0, the Blazers were no longer the league's best-kept secret. Their exploits were no longer confined to the small-market Pacific Northwest.

On this night, their first-quarter pyrotechnics were broadcast nationally and internationally via NBA Radio.

Frank Layden, the former Utah coach, was doing color commentary for the network, and he had plenty to say: "That's the best quarter I've seen in my 15 years in the league. Everything went for them. We tend to think of performances like this as 'Wow, the offense did it.' But great defense made that happen. It was a spectacular performance."

(below) Terry Porter and Rick Adelman study the game plan.
(opposite) A BlazerManiac in the making.

Terry Porter enjoys his pre-game breakfast in his Houston hotel room.

In that almost flawless first quarter, the Blazers put on a fast-break clinic, feasting off their defense. They held the Spurs to just 34.8 percent shooting (8 of 23). They forced 8 San Antonio turnovers, hauled in 7 defensive rebounds, and blocked 5 Spurs' shots. Those defensive heroics led to 7 fast-break baskets and 5 dunks.

"It was a coach's dream," said the Blazers' Buck Williams afterward. "It was like a clinic on how to play the game. I've never seen a better quarter. We just did everything right: made shots, penetrated, rebounded, got back on defense."

As sensational as that first 12 minutes of nearly perfect basketball was, the Blazers were anything but flawless for the rest of the game. They hit just 6 of 25 shots during a 15-point second quarter, as the Spurs battled back to make a game of it. Portland eventually won by a not-so-glitzy 117–103 score to earn their record-breaking 11th straight win to start a season.

No matter how lackluster the ending, though, this was a game that Blazer fans will always remember, one of those rare moments in basketball at any level when a team could hardly miss a shot for trying.

The Trail Blazers were the most dominant team in the NBA in 1990–91. They won 19 of their first 20 games and wound up breezing through March and April with 16 straight wins and a club-record 63 victories. On February 22, George Washington's birthday, the Blazers couldn't tell a lie: They were 44–10, outscoring their opponents by 10.2 points per game.

In a season like that, in which little went wrong, it would be difficult to define a turning point. Yet, looking back, the Blazers' 130–124 triple-overtime win over the Seattle Sonics at Seattle, December 1, 1990, was destiny calling. And destiny's child, in this instance, was Terry Porter.

In what was clearly the most exciting regular-season game of the most successful season in Blazer history, Porter was touched by an angel. How else could anyone explain his miracle 3-point shot that kept the Blazers alive at the end of the first overtime? Down 3 points with two seconds left, Porter took the inbounds pass. He was fouled twice by the ball-hawking Sonics, but the referees chose not to call it. Then, after bobbling the ball, he had the presence of mind to just shove it up in desperation toward the hoop. Swish!

Porter's 3-pointer tied the game at 106–106, giving the Blazers life and enough renewed energy to outlast the Sonics through two more hectic overtimes. That game was the most improbable Portland victory in the Rick Adelman era. "That game, to me, was the best one we've ever had in the regular season," Adelman said years later. "We had it won twice, and we lost it three or four times. I just didn't ever know what was going to happen next."

What happened next was a disappointment. On the way to their second NBA championship, the Blazers stumbled in the Western Conference championship series, losing to the Los Angeles Lakers, 4–2.

The Laker series revealed a Portland vulnerability: When Drexler, Porter, or both were having off games, as they did in the Laker victories in Games 3 and 4 in Los Angeles, Portland had little in the way of firepower to replace them with off the bench, Petrovic's availability notwithstanding.

So, in the off-season, Geoff Petrie, the newly appointed senior vice president for operations, and Adelman, one of his best friends since they were teammates on the 1970–73

"ENDURE THE PRESENT, AND WATCH FOR BETTER THINGS."

—VIRGIL, *THE AENEID*

(above) Danny Ainge scraps for the loose ball.
(opposite) Rick Adelman is somber after a tough loss to the Lakers in the 1991 Western Conference Finals.

Blazers, acquired veteran shooting guard Danny Ainge from Sacramento. He, in essence, became the team's productive sixth man. This didn't set well with Petrovic, who thought he should be that No. 1 bench guy. Eventually, Petrie shipped the disgruntled Petrovic to New Jersey in a three-way trade that brought veteran All-Star Walter Davis to the Blazers from Denver.

These changes were enough to propel the Blazers to a 57–25 record (second best in the league) and their shot at winning a second NBA championship. This time, though, the Blazers drew the Lakers in the playoffs right off the bat, disposing of them, 3–1, while outscoring L.A. by more than 20 points per game in their three wins.

Next up: the Phoenix Suns, a more formidable opponent than the Lakers and one that the Blazers had not beaten in Phoenix's Veterans Memorial Coliseum since the 1990 playoffs two years earlier.

It was during this series that the Blazers played probably the most memorable game in the history of the franchise. Indeed, just about every fan in the NBA can scan the

(left) Kevin Duckworth's broken right hand doesn't stop him from defending San Antonio's David Robison. *(opposite)* Drazen Petrovic

record books and recall a dream game—a larger-than-life drama with so many climaxes, so many tense moments, and so many highlights that it simply wears you out.

Eventually, the dream game becomes a part of the league's oral history—a game for the ages, not merely one for the books. Etched in memory, the dream-game story is handed down from one generation to another, no doubt embellished along the way, as storytellers lose touch with reality.

Nevertheless, these dream games hang around. They're moments in time that, when retold, seem more like fiction than fact. The Trail Blazers were part of one of these unforgettable sagas May 11, 1992, in the fourth game of the Western Conference semifinals. For the record, the Blazers prevailed over the Suns, 153–151, in double overtime. Moreover, it was the highest-scoring game in NBA playoff history and certainly one of the most exciting ever played.

It was three hours, 32 minutes of intense, chest-to-chest combat, in which just about everything imaginable went right and then wrong and then right again for the Blazers. In all, there were 22 lead changes and 20 ties.

Kevin Duckworth, who that season was the forgotten man in Portland's talent-rich starting lineup, turned out to be the hero in the second overtime, scoring 8 of his 14 points, including 4 clutch free throws in the final 43.6 seconds to clinch the victory. Yet,

this epic performance had so many climaxes, so many heroes-turned-to-goats-turned-to-heroes again, that it would be difficult to know where to start to tell the story. Besides, the thousands of Portland fans who saw it on television have their own visions of what simply should be referred to henceforth as the Game.

Clyde Drexler, among the Blazer stars, with 33 points, 11 assists, 4 rebounds, and 3 blocked shots in 51 minutes, summed up how the victorious Blazers felt about the marathon: "That kind of game is what the sport is all about. That's what makes it so much fun. That's as good as it gets." Drexler's comments were not hyperbole. They were, if anything, an understatement.

Blazer guard Danny Ainge, who contributed 25 points on 9 of 14 shooting, including four 3-pointers, compared this victory in magnitude to two of the greatest clutch victories in Boston Celtics history—two dream games that happened while Ainge was a Celtic. Blazer coach Rick Adelman said the game ranked with Portland's 1990 seventh-game playoff win over San Antonio as the two most exciting games of his career as a player or a coach, which, up to then, had spanned 17 years.

Then Phoenix president Jerry Colangelo said the game reminded him of Boston's triple-overtime win over the Suns in the 1978 NBA playoffs—the so-called Garfield Heard game, in which the Suns' journeyman Heard sent the game into overtime by sinking a desperation 20-foot shot at the buzzer. "This game and that Heard game," a drenched Colangelo told the *Oregonian*'s Kerry Eggers afterward, "were the greatest games ever played in our club's history."

For the game, Porter scored 31 points on 10 of 16 floor shooting, but uncharacteristically, he also missed 5 of 15 free throws. Porter's archrival, Kevin Johnson, matched Porter step for step, with 35 points and 14 assists. Their personal battle proved to be yet another great subplot of this passion play.

The Suns took a 149–146 lead in the second overtime on Cedric Ceballos's layup with 1:15 to go. That's when Duckworth came to the Blazers' rescue. Kevin had scored only 6 points through the regulation and the first overtime. But he scored two of

Portland's first 3 field goals in the second overtime on short hook shots, then drained 4 straight foul shots with the game hanging in the balance. His first two gave the Blazers a 150–149 lead with 43.6 seconds left.

After Dan Majerle's 15-footer with 27.3 seconds left gave the Suns the lead again, Duckworth rebounded a Drexler miss, was fouled, and converted two more with 10.7 seconds left. "My biggest moment in basketball," said Duckworth after the game. "You know how you felt after you had your first kid? This is it for me. This is the best so far."

"This one is so satisfying," said Adelman afterward. "We just refused to quit. It was one of those games for the archives. I'll never forget this game. I doubt if anyone who saw it back home or any of the players who played in it will ever forget it, either."

Three days later, the Blazers finished off the Suns at home, 118–106, behind Drexler's 34 points, then claimed the Western Conference championship in a bruising six-game series against Utah in which Terry Porter and Jerome Kersey played starring roles. Those heroics earned Portland a second trip to the NBA Finals in three seasons, this time against the league's best—the Chicago Bulls.

Sometimes it pays to ignore the trends, buck the odds, reject conventional wisdom, disregard the handwriting on the scoreboard—and forget that Michael Jordan is on the other team. Such was the challenge for the Trail Blazers June 5, 1992, in Game 2 of the NBA championship series against the Chicago Bulls.

Yet this night produced one of those unexplainable finishes that TV commentators have a hard time digesting, let alone analyzing. It was like a whodunit mystery in which all the clues point to the butler, but it turns out the family dog did it.

Jordan was having another great game—39 points. The Bulls were in total control of the Blazers for more than 43 minutes, taking a 10-point lead with just 4:25 remaining to be played. The humiliating 33-point loss to the Bulls at Chicago Stadium in Game 1, in which Jordan put on a Hall of Fame performance, with a record-breaking 35 first-half points, embarrassed the Blazers. It was difficult enough for Blazer fans to accept such an unexpected drubbing in the opener, but to endure TV replays of Jordan's 3-point barrage (he hit 6 long bombs in the first half of Game 1) and his sheepish smile and shrug of the shoulders as he stared at the cameraman, as if to say, "Hey, I'm in a little zone here," was scary stuff.

So in Game 2, when Chicago blitzed the Blazers, 32–16, in the third period to take a 77–70 lead, even loyal Blazer fans may have thought about changing horses. Predictably, too, the pundits on ESPN and NBC, who always seem to ride shotgun on the winning bandwagons of the day, were starting to speculate that the Bulls would easily sweep Portland in four games.

And to make matters worse, Portland's All-Star and best player, Clyde Drexler, had just fouled out, taking his Portland-high 26 points to the bench with him. So inquiring Bulls fans wanted to know: How could the Blazers possibly win the second game of this series, especially after the Bulls had thoroughly annihilated them, 122–89, just two nights earlier?

They got their answer soon enough. The Bulls scored only 3 points in the final four minutes of regulation and were blown out in overtime, with Phil Jackson's vaunted defense crumbling before a Portland offense that started moving the ball and driving to the basket.

Terry Porter, who finished with 24 points, directed Portland's offense so efficiently that it scored on 16 of its last 17 possessions. Meanwhile, the previously unstoppable Mr. Jordan was proving himself to be mortal—his chariot fireless. "Michael's cape fell off there somewhere down the stretch," said Danny Ainge, who scored 9 of his 17 points in the overtime period, tying an NBA finals record.

The unforeseen Blazer turnaround in Game 2 knotted the series at 1–1, with Portland gaining home-court advantage and heading back home for three games. Hearts were light in Rip City for the next few days, and basketball pundits the world over were jumping on the Blazer bandwagon. Like modern-day Ferdinand Magellans, they boasted of discovering the Trail Blazers.

The euphoria didn't last, though. In sports, you just can't ignore the trends, or the odds, or conventional wisdom, or the handwriting on the scoreboard for too long—and, in 1992, the team with Michael Jordan on it eventually ruled, winning the series, 4–2.

The window of opportunity, sad to say, was beginning to close for this Blazer team. Ainge left town the next season for Phoenix, but Petrie signed free agent Rod Strickland, one of the best pure point guards the Blazers ever had (he still holds the franchise record for assists in a game, 20, which he did twice, against Phoenix in 1994 and at Houston in 1996).

Strickland helped the 1992–93 Blazers reach a respectable 51–31 record, but injuries to Drexler, who missed 33 games, and Kersey, out for 17 more, were a sign that the great ones of 1990–92 had grown older. Portland slipped to 47–35 the next year, dropping out of the first round of the playoffs, without much resistance, for the second year in a row.

At the start of the 1993–94 season, Cliff Robinson, in his fifth year, emerged as Portland's best player. Seattle coach George Karl anointed Uncle Cliffy with that honor when he said, "I've said it before and I'll say it again: He's their best player right now. You have to give Clyde Drexler his respect, but from the standpoint of just a point-blank player, Cliff has done more for Portland's team the past two years than anybody else."

Indiana coach Larry Brown seconded that notion: "Last season, he went from winning the league's Sixth Man award to a legitimate place on the league's All-Star team." Yet even the fast-rising Robinson couldn't keep that championship window open.

Ever-hopeful fans didn't know it then, but the Blazers sorely needed a major overhaul, and by the end of 1994 they officially ended the Rick Adelman and Geoff Petrie era and turned the keys to Rip City over to "Trader" Bob Whitsitt.

Cliff Robinson (left) and Mark Bryant (right) celebrate as Alaa Abdelnaby (center) looks on.

Bill Schonely, the Trail Blazers' voice and goodwill ambassador since Day One.

CLYDE THE GLIDE

BY KERRY EGGERS

He experienced the absolute highs of his profession: An Olympic gold medal with the original Dream Team in 1992. An NBA championship with the Houston Rockets in 1995. Induction into the Naismith Basketball Hall of Fame in 2004.

His biggest accomplishment in the game? That's easy, says Clyde Drexler. "Putting on that Trail Blazer jersey for the first time. Making it to the NBA was my lifetime dream."

Retired and working as a part-time analyst for the Rockets television broadcasts, Drexler, now 48, spent more than 11 of his 15 NBA seasons wearing No. 22 for a Portland franchise that, quite simply, wouldn't have been the same without him. The Houston native holds club career records in many categories, including scoring (18,040), rebounds (5,339), and steals (1,795). More than that, though, Drexler remains a hallowed player whose legend remains untarnished through time.

Asked for his fondest memory about his years in Portland—from 1984, when he was taken with the 14th pick of the draft, to 1995, when he was traded to Houston in a midseason deal—Drexler recalls his love affair with BlazerMania. "Every day, being able to be in a great city like Portland, which enabled me to develop at my own pace," he says. "And having the support of the fans. I still think they're the best fans in the NBA to this day. To have that support behind you is phenomenal. They love the game and they love the team. It provided a nurturing environment that was perfect for a young player like myself, trying to develop as both a person and a player. They were always loyal, always forgiving, and they showed up in record numbers. Even after the losses, they were faithful. There's a lot to be said for that."

Born in New Orleans to James and Eunice Drexler, Clyde moved to Houston at age three with his mother when his parents split up. Clyde was the last of three children by his parents, but Eunice had seven kids in all, with Clyde in the middle of three boys and four girls, who were raised in a lower-middle-class home—a ten-minute drive from the University of Houston campus.

Eunice worked checking groceries, then began running a family restaurant in 1982. Clyde's stepfather, Manuel, was a butcher by trade, and had an alcohol problem that left Clyde, at times, walking on eggshells around him. His oldest brother, Michael, got into drugs and, at age 18, was shot by police and killed while trying to rob a pharmacy when Clyde was 11. There were plenty of chances to get into trouble during his formative years, but Clyde mostly avoided them, thanks in no small part

"We were going to smoke dope and chase women, and he was always practicing his game," his childhood friend Craig "Twin" Lewis says. "I respect him for that."

"We all inherently know what's right and wrong," Drexler says. "If you choose to do something productive with your life, you try to do the things that are conducive to that. It's all about making good decisions. Life is a series of choices. If you make bad ones, there are consequences. If you make good ones, you have a chance to succeed."

Eunice Drexler, now 75 and retired from the family barbecue restaurant, which she finally closed in 2006, deserves plenty of credit for her guidance as well. "My mom has been a rock of support, the person most responsible for what I've done with my life," Drexler says. "She is my mother, but she is also my best friend."

When he started his freshman year at Sterling High, Clyde was 5-foot-8 and served as the 13th man on the freshman team that season. He never let that get him down. "I don't think I was smart enough to be discouraged, to be honest," he says with a laugh. "I was involved with school, had my friends, was trying to be like every other kid. And I really enjoyed basketball. I didn't like not getting to play much on my team, but that was motivation to get better."

Drexler grew in a hurry. By January of his sophomore year, he was 6-foot-4, but didn't play for the school team that season because he had the flu during junior-varsity tryouts. He started on the varsity as a 6-foot-7 center as a junior and senior, "but Clyde was just part of a good team," teammate Joe Cotton says. "His emergence as a player really came between high school and college. There were a lot of guys who could have been Clyde Drexler. He was the one guy who capitalized on his opportunity."

With little recruiting interest from major colleges, Drexler signed with hometown Houston as part of a package deal with good friend Michael Young, the state's Player of the Year at a rival high school and a *Parade* All-American. Clyde became the better player at UH, teaming with Hakeem Olajuwon to lead Phi Slama Jama to a pair of Final Fours.

A first-team All-American and Southwest Conference Player of the Year, Drexler entered the NBA draft after his junior year and was promised by Houston general manager Ray Patterson he would be taken by the Rockets with the third pick. But coach Del Harris was fired and replaced by Bill Fitch, who liked

Clyde Drexler soars against the New Jersey Nets.

Drexler had gone to only one pre draft workout with an individual team—Portland, which held the 14th pick. Blazer execs Stu Inman and Bucky Buckwalter convinced coach Jack Ramsay that Drexler was their guy.

"We didn't have a need at either small forward or shooting guard, but Stu and Bucky were very high on Clyde," Ramsay says. "He was simply the best player available. It was Stu's pick, and he chose Clyde."

Drexler was drafted right behind Ennis Whatley, who was taken by Sacramento at No. 13. Among others who went before Drexler were Steve Stipanovich, No. 2, to Indiana, and Russell Cross, No. 6, to Golden State. Drexler never forgot the teams that bypassed him in the draft.

"You make a mental note," Drexler says. "I tried to torture those teams every chance I got the rest of my career. Being a competitive person, you don't say anything, but you definitely remember."

Drexler held out and didn't sign a contract until the week before the regular season began. He began the season playing behind Darnell Valentine at point guard, Jim Paxson at shooting guard, and Calvin Natt at small forward, but before long, teammate Mychal Thompson was calling the Blazers "Clyde's team."

Still, Ramsay rarely started rookies, and he wasn't about to start Drexler. Drexler sought him out in December, saying if he didn't get 25 to 30 minutes a game by the All-Star break, he would ask for a trade.

"Clyde, you know you have a couple of All-Stars ahead of you," Ramsay said. "I can't just put you in front of them."

"Why not?" was Drexler's response.

A little while later, Drexler did ask for a trade. "But I was really trying to force Jack's hand to play me more," he says now. Paxson held out before Drexler's second season and Drexler moved into his starting spot, with Kiki Vandeweghe at small forward. After Paxson signed, Drexler played a lot of point guard and started 42 games, and by his third season was an All-Star. "Clyde had his own way of playing, and Jack eventually accepted it," Thompson says. "You can't turn Secretariat into a plow horse."

"Jack was one of those coaches who made you earn it," Drexler says. "Even after you prove yourself, you still have to wait. But when I look back, I wouldn't have had it any other way. He was perfect, the greatest coach in the world to develop a young, stubborn player like myself. He challenged you every day." Drexler emerged as one of the game's greats under Rick Adelman, who had joined Ramsay's staff as an assistant coach during Drexler's rookie year. They were to have five standout seasons together, getting to the NBA Finals in 1990 and '92.

"By the time Rick became the head coach [in 1989], we had talent and just needed a couple of more pieces," Drexler says. "We added Cliff [Robinson] and Buck [Williams] to go along with the nucleus, and suddenly we were rolling. I was kind of sad that year, because we had gotten rid of Kiki and Steve [Johnson], two of my really good friends who were also great players. But I could tell we were starting a new era, one that was going to be more successful."

(above) Clyde Drexler acknowledges the crowd after winning the gold medal with the original Dream Team at the 1992 Barcelona Olympics. (opposite) Clyde Drexler dunks on Patrick Ewing during the 1992 NBA All-Star Game in Orlando.

Adelman brought out the best in Drexler, and put up with the things that had bothered his predecessors, Ramsay and Mike Schuler. "Rick knew everything about me," Drexler says. "He knew my strengths. He never talked about what we couldn't do. He talked about what we need to do. As a player, you couldn't help but love him. He gave you everything you needed to succeed."

Over three seasons, 1990–92, Portland averaged nearly 60 wins, won two Western Conference titles, and made at least the conference finals all three years. In 1990–91, the Blazers finished with a league-best 63–19 regular-season record, only to lose to Magic Johnson and the Lakers in the West finals. "We were the best team in the league for those three years—I truly believe that," Drexler says.

He thinks NBA executives and officials made it difficult on the Blazers, desiring teams in larger markets such as Detroit, Chicago, and Los Angeles to win titles. "I don't think the league was ready for it back then," Drexler says. San Antonio finally broke the mold in 1999. "There were some intangibles to overcome in a small market like Portland. The league wanted the Michael/Magic matchup [in the '91 Finals].

Before the 1991–92 season, Drexler signed a one-year contract extension for $9.75 million—to be paid for the 1995–96 season—the largest one-year salary of any pro athlete in any sport to that point. He was at the height of his career during the All-Star game that season, when he had 22 points, 9 rebounds, and 6 assists in 28 minutes for the winning West team and seemed a good bet to win the Most Valuable Player award.

But Magic Johnson—who had announced before the season that he had HIV, retired from the game, and then was added to the West All-Star roster—was a sentimental choice. With Drexler feeding his teammate, Magic had a huge fourth quarter and earned the MVP award, getting nine votes to two for Drexler. "In that situation, I'd have voted for him, too," Drexler said with a laugh.

During the '92 playoffs, Drexler got word that he was the last professional being added to the Dream Team. With players such as Jordan, Johnson, Larry Bird, Charles Barkley, Scottie Pippen, John Stockton, Karl Malone, David Robinson, and Patrick Ewing, Clyde etched his name on a team that history will never forget.

Things went downhill in Portland, in part due to injuries to Drexler. After first-round playoff ousters in 1993 and '94, General Manager Bob Whitsitt sent Drexler to Houston for Otis Thorpe plus a first-round pick on Valentine's Day 1995, agreeing additionally to cover about $7 million of Clyde's $9.75 million payment for the 1995–96 campaign. Four months later, Drexler was riding in a parade in his hometown, celebrating an NBA championship. Drexler missed out on some national endorsement opportunities by playing in a small market in Portland. He says he has never regretted that.

"Portland was the team that had the faith to draft me," he says. "There might have been more marketing opportunities in larger cities like New York or L.A., or even Chicago or Boston, but other teams passed me by. I was more than happy to play in Portland." Today, Drexler is regarded as the second-best shooting guard of his era, behind Jordan. Drexler has his own spin on that.

"That's a compliment, because Michael was really good," he says. "To be considered the second-greatest two guard of my era is a magnificent accomplishment, but we had different mentalities. Michael was a 30-shot-a-game guy. My attitude was pass first. I was a playmaker. If I needed to score, I could always score. But just think if I had a score-30-points-a-night mentality. Had I been interested in padding my stats, oh my goodness."

When career numbers in scoring, rebounds, assists, and steals are combined, Drexler ranks fifth among NBA guards with 37,204, behind Jordan (47,111), Oscar Robertson (44,478), John Stockton (42,933), and Gary Payton (38,493).

"I was never a specialist," Drexler says. "I always tried to play an all-around game. Give credit to my coaches. They never told me what I couldn't do. They allowed me the opportunity to do what I could do."

Kerry Eggers is a sports columnist for the *Portland Tribune*.

CROSSROADS

CHAPTER 6

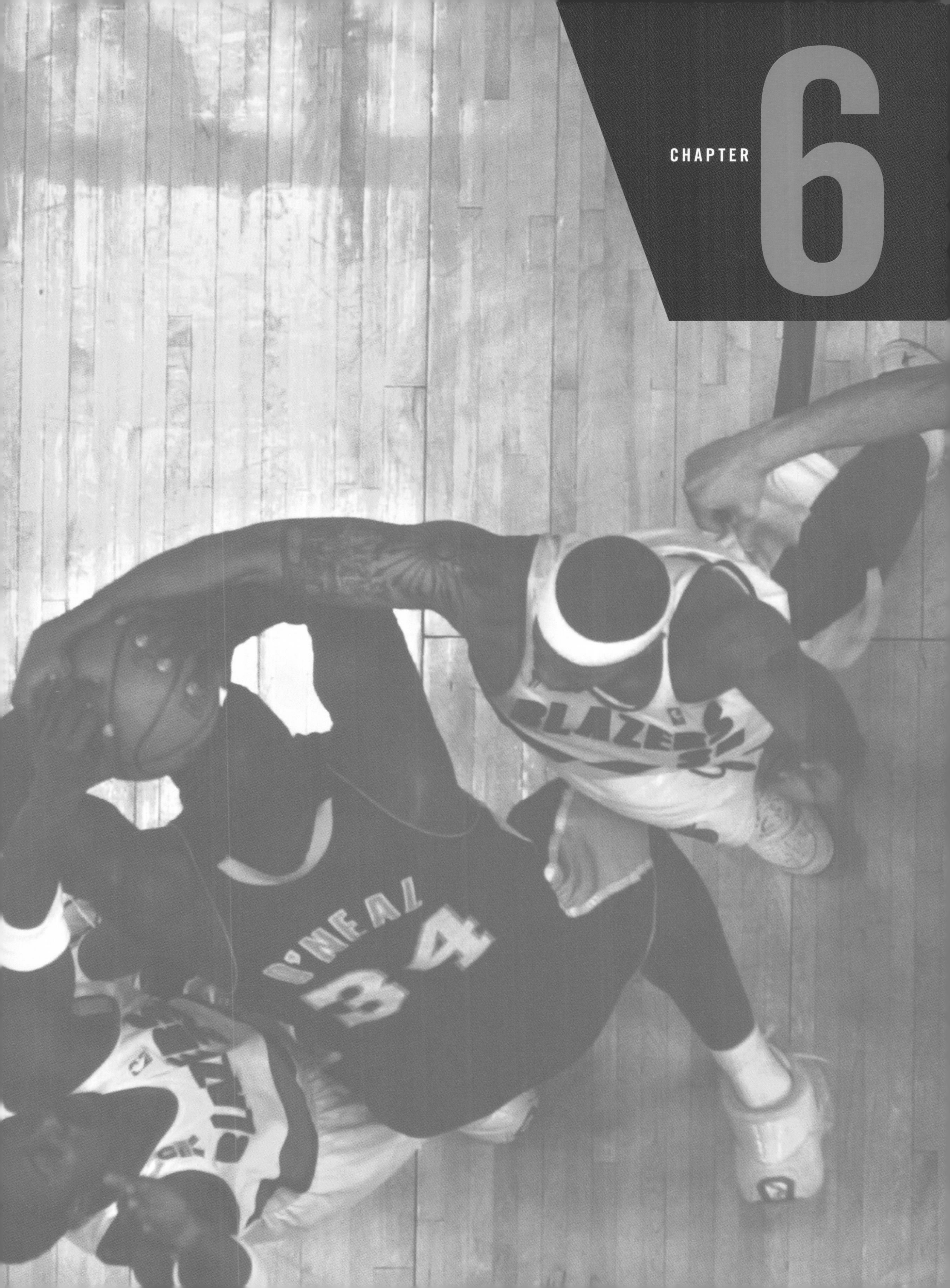

"IF I HAD ASKED PEOPLE WHAT
THEY WANTED, THEY WOULD
HAVE SAID
FASTER HORSES."

—HENRY FORD

When Bob Whitsitt became the president and general manager of the Trail Blazers in 1994, it marked a crossroads not only for the team, but for the fans as well. It was a time of transition, from the old—the Adelman-Drexler era—to the unknown: How could Whitsitt build the Blazers into a **contender** again—and quickly?

(above) Bob Whitsitt
(opposite) Arvydas Sabonis shoots a hook shot over the LA Lakers' Shaquille O'Neal.
(previous spread) The Blazers battle O'Neal in the paint.

He could build the team the way the great Blazer clubs of the late 1970s and the early 1990s did, by relying mostly on the draft. But that would take time and no doubt guarantee that the Blazers would finish out of the playoffs for a few years.

The other way he could do it would be to wheel and deal, placing great emphasis on acquiring underutilized talent but ignoring some of the reasons why such talent was undervalued.

This was the tradeoff—either choose to grow the team up from scratch, through a youth movement that would balance a player's character with his talent, or make trades and sign free agents that other teams didn't want, while managing the league's salary cap to keep the team in the playoff hunt for as long as possible.

The latter, make no mistake, was the prudent, less painful way to go about it. And it would appease the fans, who surely didn't want their Blazers to fall to the bottom of the heap like almost all rebuilding teams in the NBA, including the Lakers (1991–94) and the Celtics (1993–2001, 2005–07), have had to do.

Portland ultimately chose the latter approach, which was a major reason why the Blazers' near-record streak of making it to the playoffs for 21 straight years stayed alive during the Whitsitt era.

Whitsitt was among the best executives in basketball at acquiring talented players within the rigid limits of the league's salary cap—the 1999 trade with Houston for Scottie Pippen is the best example.

Dozens of Whitsitt moves over the course of 10 years brought Rasheed Wallace, Isaiah J. R. Rider, Kenny Anderson, Damon Stoudamire, Walt Williams, Jim Jackson, Steve Smith, Bonzi Wells, Detlef Schrempf, Brian Grant, Shawn Kemp, Dale Davis, and Derek Anderson to Portland—moves that were lauded at the time by Blazer fans who looked forward each year to keeping Portland's winning tradition alive.

(left) Owner Paul Allen, Trail Blazers president Marshall Glickman, and NBA commissioner David Stern raise glasses during the Rose Garden's grand opening ceremonies November 3, 1995.
(below and opposite) The Rose Garden takes shape.

Some of these players, however, were available on the market at bargain prices partly because of suspected character issues, but most all of them, except for Kemp, perhaps, proved in Portland that they could play. Though this strategy eventually led to the so-called Jail Blazer era, most fans were somewhat content with it, at first, so long as the Blazers were contenders for a title (the 1999–2000 Blazers best exemplify this strategy; they were one of the most talented Blazer teams ever—on paper, at least).

Many critics say that Whitsitt would have been the quintessential general manager of a fantasy team, where players are selected based on their individual skills and stats rather than on how they would actually play together on a team. In contrast to Stu Inman and Bucky Buckwalter before him, Whitsitt, his critics claim, placed little value on team chemistry.

Nevertheless, in his 10 years as president and general manager, Whitsitt's teams had a win-loss record of 426–280, a winning percentage second only to Bucky Buckwalter's, among all the talent hunters the Blazers have ever had.

Of course, there were exceptions: Brian Grant, acquired by Whitsitt in 1997 as a free agent, proved to be a player with the biggest heart and will to win of all the Blazers. Fans will recall his bloody battles with Utah's rugged Karl Malone in the 2000 playoffs.

The Blazer who perhaps stood the tallest in the Whitsitt era was Arvydas Sabonis, the 7-foot-3 Lithuanian center acquired in the 1986 college draft, eight years before Whitsitt joined the Blazers. Ex-NBA players and current players alike contend that Sabonis, little known in the United States when Portland selected him as a 31-year-old, would have been recognized as one of the top centers ever to play the game had he come to America in his prime.

(above) Longtime Blazers fan (opposite) Brian Grant (center) drives past Houston's Scottie Pippen (left) and Charles Barkley (right).

Scottie Pippen said that Arvydas was "the best European basketball player ever to play the game." Former San Antonio forward Sean Elliott routinely claimed that Arvydas "should be in the conversation as one of the greatest centers ever." And Hall of Famer Bill Walton describes Sabonis as "the greatest passing center of all time."

The late Brian Meehan, a columnist for the *Oregonian*, followed Sabonis's career over the course of decades. Recalling the 1988 Olympics, when Sabonis's Soviet team beat an amateur United States team whose stars were David Robinson and Mitch Richmond, Meehan noted that on one play, a healthy 23-year-old Sabonis reacted to a teammate's missed shot, slashed toward the rim, and slammed the ball home, thus "posterizing" a future Hall of Famer, David Robinson. It was that image of Arvydas dunking over Robinson in the 1988 Olympics, Meehan believed, that influenced Team USA to use professional players in the Olympics, hence the Dream Teams of 1992 and '96.

Coming to the Blazers in 1995 as a 31-year-old rookie (a move made possible by owner Paul Allen's perseverance in aggressively pursing him for seven years), Sabonis had several mind-blowing games, but none more memorable than the one on February 25, 1998, when the Blazers upset the fabled Chicago Bulls, 106–101. Playing on wounded knees at the age of 33, Arvydas scored 21 points and hauled down 20 rebounds, tying his NBA-season rebound high, which he had set a month earlier against Denver. He was a force throughout. In a rare postgame interview, Sabonis made it clear that this game would have special prominence in his scrapbook. "The win is important for us, especially against Chicago. The Bulls are such a good team. It's important for me, for my kids, to know in the years to come that we beat them."

Paul Allen celebrates a Blazers victory with Bill and Melinda Gates.
Allen and Gates co-founded Microsoft in 1975.

P. J. Carlesimo goes over the game plan with Chris Dudley, Arvydas Sabonis, Buck Williams, and Rod Strickland.

The Bulls had been on a roll, having won 26 of 28 games in the United Center in this, their final go at the NBA championship. Entering the game, Chicago (42–16) had won eight in a row since the All-Star break and was headed for the NBA's best season record for the third straight year. Led by Michael Jordan and Scottie Pippen, the Bulls seemed invincible: They were Sherman with a blowtorch and the league was Georgia.

For all their talent, though, the Bulls simply couldn't cope with the player that Chicago coach Phil Jackson grudgingly called "just a mountain of a man who in his prime may have been the most skilled offensive center around." Sabonis's milestone victory over the Bulls in Chicago—the one he said he would share with his children in his golden years—was the beginning of a dozen great games for the quiet Lithuanian. It started February 22, with a 23-point, 11-rebound display in a win at Boston, carried over to Chicago, and continued for 10 more games into mid-March. It was highlighted by a 28-point, 20-rebound domination of the Minnesota Timberwolves, and culminated in a 21-point, 11-rebound performance in a Blazer win at New York. This stretch of games, in which Arvydas averaged 22 points and 17 rebounds, was the best month of basketball he ever played in the NBA. It was a defining moment for him because it showed basketball fans throughout the nation what all the basketball insiders in Europe and America already knew: that Arvydas Sabonis, even though he was beyond his prime and operating on bad wheels, could really play this game.

oward the end of the Whitsitt era and extending into the Steve Patterson–John Nash regime, the Blazers produced more negatives than positives. This began to embarrass Portland's loyal fans as they were reading more stories about players' bad behavior off the court than their stellar performances on it. Thus, the Jail Blazers— poorly named in the sense that no Blazer spent significant time in jail—were born. That is to say that Isaiah J. R. Rider, Zach Randolph, Qyntel Woods, Gary Trent, Ruben Patterson, Bonzi Wells, and Rasheed Wallace weren't exactly choirboys, but they were good players regardless of their transgressions. In spite of these franchise-diminishing incidents, the Whitsitt teams of the early 21st century were fun to watch as dozens of really talented players trickled in and out of the locker room while wheeler-dealer Whitsitt seemed to capitalize on every opportunity to land talented, if sometimes misguided, players.

Whitsitt changed Blazer coaches almost as often as he revamped the roster. P. J. Carlesimo, who had a 137–109 win-loss record in three seasons, Mike Dunleavy, whose 190–106 mark in four seasons is the greatest winning percentage (64.2 percent)

(this page, clockwise from top) Trail Blazers coaches: Maurice Cheeks; P. J. Carlesimo; Mike Dunleavy

of any coach in Blazer history, and Maurice Cheeks, who won 162 games in almost four seasons (and was fired by John Nash, March 4, 2005) did only one thing wrong: Except for Dunleavy from 1998 to 2000, they never got Portland out of the first round of the playoffs. Dunleavy's sin: His 1999–2000 team, which won 59 games, blew a 15-point lead with less than a quarter left to play in the seventh game of the Western Conference Finals, thus depriving Portland of reaching the NBA finals for the fourth time.

Clearly the gemstone of the Whitsitt era was the 1999–2000 Blazers, a team with so much firepower and star power that it would probably receive some votes as one of the greatest NBA teams ever assembled—on paper, that is. On the court and in the clutch, not so much.

The roster of the great team that ushered in the 21st century includes Rasheed Wallace, Steve Smith, Brian Grant, Arvydas Sabonis, Scottie Pippen, Damon Stoudamire, Bonzi Wells, Detlef Schrempf, Jermaine O'Neal, Greg Anthony, Stacey Augmon, Joe Kleine, and Antonio Harvey—it was loaded with talent, for sure, but perhaps it was overloaded, too deep to keep everyone happy and everyone sharp.

(below) Jermaine O'Neal with the stuff against the Washington Bullets

Here is just a sample of the player power that explains why this team, in spite of its failure in the playoffs, was perhaps the greatest collection of talent ever assembled by the Blazers:

• Scottie Pippen, one of the top 50 players in the first half century of the NBA, a member of the 1992 Olympic Dream Team, and recently inducted into the Basketball Hall of Fame, was acquired by the Blazers from Houston in October 1999. Whitsitt sent six Blazers (Stacey Augmon, Kelvin Cato, Ed Gray, Carlos Rogers, Brian Shaw, and Walt Williams) to the Rockets for Pippen, and then re-signed Augmon, a talented defensive forward, when Houston released him. Ironically, it was Brian Shaw who turned out to be one of the heroes in L.A.'s fourth-quarter comeback in Game 7 of the Western Conference finals that ended Portland's run.

• Rasheed Wallace, a two-time All-Star and one of the best young power forwards in the NBA, spent eight seasons with the Blazers. He was acquired by Whitsitt in July 1996 from Washington in exchange for Harvey Grant and Rod Strickland. At the time, the national media considered this a steal, enhancing Whitsitt's reputation as a shrewd dealmaker.

• Damon Stoudamire, Portland native and former Rookie of the Year in Toronto, was acquired by Whitsitt in 1998 in a multiplayer trade, the Blazers sending Kenny Anderson, Gary Trent, Alvin Williams, two first-round draft choices, and one second-round choice to the Raptors. Mighty Mouse, only 5-foot-9, was one of Portland's greatest shooters and scoring point guards ever. (Note: Over the Blazers' 40 years, team management seemed to be attracted to southpaw point guards, as illustrated by this list: Stoudamire, Greg Anthony—star of the 1991 NCAA-champion UNLV Rebels—Nick Van Exel, Kenny Anderson, Lionel Hollins, Lenny Wilkens, Dennis Layton, Rick Brunson, and John Crotty.)

• Steve Smith, a U.S. Olympic gold medalist in 2000, and one of the league's top shooting guards in the 1990s, was acquired by Whitsitt in August 1999 from Atlanta for guards Isaiah Rider and Jim Jackson. Smitty, in just two seasons with the Blazers, was selected as one of the top 40 Blazers of all time by the *Oregonian*.

• Detlef Schrempf, a versatile forward in his 14th NBA season, and a star in the Seattle Sonics' winning seasons in the '90s, was one of Whitsitt's favorites. Signed in 1999 as a free agent, Detlef was allowed to commute to Blazer practices from his home in Seattle, some 175 miles from Portland. This seemed reasonable to Whitsitt, himself a Seattle resident who did the same commute, but it suggested a troubling double standard to Dunleavy and the team.

• Other notables on that special team—Arvydas Sabonis (mentioned earlier); Brian Grant, a star at Xavier and later at Sacramento, who became Portland's tough-minded defensive stopper; Bonzi Wells, one of Whitsitt's best draft-day deals; and Jermaine O'Neal, the talented high schooler whose career was yet to bloom—had been, or were soon to be, very good players in the league.

(above) Jimmy Jackson (left) and J. R. Rider (right) celebrate a victory in the Western Conference Semifinals versus San Antonio. Portland took the series, 4–2.
(opposite) Rasheed Wallace and referee Joey Crawford exchange pleasantries.

But during the 1999–2000 season, in spite of all the off-season deal making, Portland opened by winning 10 of its first 11 games. Later, the Blazers had two winning streaks of six straight games and another in which they won 11 games in a row to post a record of 45–11. But down the stretch, the Blazers became lethargic and a bit overconfident, closing out the regular season by winning only 14 of their final 26 games.

Of those losses, the one that hurt the most was the final game, a 96–95 home loss to Denver, which prevented the Blazers from posting the franchise's second 60-win season. In the 2000 playoffs that followed, the Blazers advanced to the Western Conference finals easily against Minnesota (3–1) and Utah (4–1), but suffered what most Blazer fans would agree was the most heartbreaking loss in the team's history.

Here's the way it came down: Despite losing two home games to the Lakers to fall behind 3–1 in the series, the Blazers rallied to tie the series, 3–3, with the deciding game scheduled for Los Angeles. Steve Smith, the second-leading scorer on that team, says he still has nightmares today about the way that game ended. Leading by the score of 73–58 early in the fourth quarter, Portland was outscored, 31–11, in the final 11 minutes as the Lakers, with the Blazer discard Brian Shaw canning 3-pointers at pivotal times, went on to win, 89–84.

(left) Kobe Bryant (left) and Scottie Pippen (right) battle for a loose ball.
(above, top to bottom) Scottie Pippen gives a hug to Bonzi Wells; Steve Smith; Damon Stoudamire celebrates with teammate Derek Anderson after a game-winning shot against the Seattle Supersonics at the Rose Garden on December 21, 2002.

(right) Brian Grant
(bottom) Scottie Pippen (left), Maurice Cheeks (center), and Rasheed Wallace (right) shooting pool at the Trail Blazers practice facility.

Dunleavy's team had one more chance to redeem itself, finishing the 2000–01 season with a 50–32 mark, but this time they got ousted without a whimper by the Lakers, 3–0, in the first round of the playoffs. It might have turned out differently for Dunleavy had Whitsitt not overreacted to the Blazers' loss in the 2000 Western Conference finals. He shook up a solid roster with ill-advised moves that most basketball pundits found hard to reconcile, given the strengths and depth of the 1999–2000 team. For example, he gave up Brian Grant, the heart and soul of the 59-win team, for an out-of-shape and over-the-hill Shawn Kemp, who was one of the league's great power forwards in Seattle when Whitsitt was general manager of the Sonics. Kemp had lost his quickness and his outside shot and, a year later, he ended his brief Blazer career in rehab. Another bad move was sending the promising 6-foot-11 youngster Jermaine O'Neal to Indiana for veteran forward Dale Davis, a solid defender and rebounder for the Eastern Conference–champion Indiana Pacers, but a player with limited offensive skills. O'Neal went on to become a six-time NBA All-Star.

The disappointment of not regaining the magic of 1999–2000 ended Dunleavy's tenure. His replacement, Maurice Cheeks, was a rookie coach who was often unsure about how to handle time-management and player-rotation problems. The Cheeks era was predictably unpredictable. Just when it appeared that the wheels had come off the bus for good, the Blazers seemed to surprise even themselves with a heroic effort. For example, in a spectacular game on January 22, 2003, in Atlanta, the Blazers, trying to overcome the league-imposed suspension of Rasheed Wallace, outdueled the Hawks in a double-overtime thriller, 112–110.

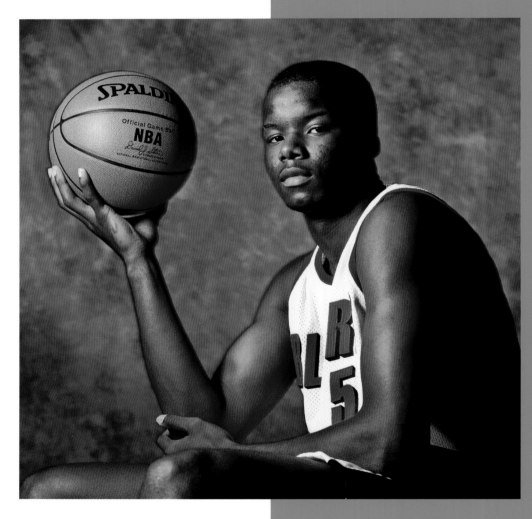

In the Atlanta win, Cheeks's Blazers, resilient and brilliant at times, yet careless and listless at others, thought they had won it, then lost it, then won it back, then blew it again. They finally did win it on Bonzi Wells's driving layup with 1.4 seconds left in the second overtime.

As the Blazer fortunes began to fade in late 2005 (the Blazers in 2004–05 were about to post their worst record in 31 years), Cheeks was let go and a new star was born, not as a coach, but as

(above) Jermaine O'Neal
(opposite) Dale Davis

a franchise builder. Before that could happen, however, the Blazers spent a couple of seasons with a new president, Steve Patterson, and a new general manager, John Nash, who worked hard to dispel Portland's bad-boy image, but accomplished little in improving their results on the court (68 wins, 95 losses).

Nash left the Blazers following the 2005–06 season, and Patterson assumed the dual role of president and general manager. Meanwhile, Kevin Pritchard was gaining influence as Portland's director of player personnel. Allen charged Patterson and Pritchard with building the Blazers through the draft, and with an equal emphasis on character and talent.

In fairness to Whitsitt, he was a very smart and creative operator who gambled that keeping Portland in the playoff hunt through trades, free agent hires, and draft picks was an efficient way to rebuild the Blazers after the Adelman teams had gotten too old and needed a major overhaul.

(left to right) Derek Anderson, Rasheed Wallace, Scottie Pippen, Dale Davis, and Damon Stoudamire watch from the bench.

During his tenure, Whitsitt got some sound basketball advice from assistant general manager Mark Warkentien. A fan of athletic players with superior jumping ability, Warkentien also could see the virtue in players like Zach Randolph, who had honed other instincts to compensate for his lack of jumping skills. Warkentien had the foresight to select Michigan State freshman and super sub Randolph with the 19th pick in the 2000 college draft. Even though Randolph had limited on-court experience, Warkentien believed that the bulky 260-pound forward, who averaged one rebound every three minutes through his prep and college careers, would duplicate those numbers in the NBA. And he was right about that. But like his boss, Whitsitt, Warkentien was more interested in a player's skill set on the court than his behavior off it. During the Whitsitt years, the acquisition of Isaiah J. R. Rider, Gary Trent, Dontonio Wingfield, Qyntel Woods, Ruben Patterson and even Randolph helped cement Portland's hard-to-shake Jail Blazer rep, to the endless embarrassment of their once-loyal fan base.

Some very lean years came to Rip City before peace, harmony, and the Blazer image were restored.

(top) Damon Stoudamire drives past the LA Lakers' Ron Harper.
(above) Rasheed Wallace leads the team huddle.

During a 2003 playoff game against the Dallas Mavericks, coach Maurice Cheeks aided 13-year-old Natalie Gilbert in singing the National Anthem after she forgot the words mid-song. Cheeks rushed to her aid and they finished it together, as the entire Rose Garden Arena crowd sang with them. Cheeks and Gilbert received a standing ovation after the song was over.

WITH ADVERSITY COMES
OPPORTUNITY

"ABILITY MAY GET YOU TO THE TOP, BUT IT TAKES **CHARACTER** TO KEEP YOU THERE."

—JOHN WOODEN

Some of the lessons learned from the Bob Whitsitt years were difficult for the Trail Blazers and their fans to swallow. That winning is not always **everything** seemed an unkind assault on the ambitions of a team that was used to competing with the best in the NBA. In the end, Blazer fans had to come to grips with the fact that producing winning records and making the playoffs every year could come at a cost to the team's personality and character. Hence, the Jail Blazers of the New Millennium.

So the lesson about winning was learned the hard way, through declining fan support and league-wide embarrassment.

The message coming down from Paul Allen was to build teams with strong character values, and it had no more enthusiastic disciple than Kevin Pritchard, who was charged with the responsibility of bringing the Trail Blazers back to respectability on the court. Larry Miller, the president of the Trail Blazers, and Sarah Mensah, the senior vice president and chief marketing officer, were key figures in restoring the Blazer brand off the court. On the way to that turning-point moment, though, the Blazers had to endure some troubling times. Their downfall began in the 2003–04 season, when Portland used a franchise-record 24 players to complete a break-even 41–41 season, missing the playoffs for the first time since 1982.

Ten straight road losses got the Blazers off to their worst start away from home since 1981. Three major trades involving starters Rasheed Wallace, Bonzi Wells, and Jeff McInnis got rid of some of the bad chemistry that coach Maurice Cheeks was dealing with on the court, but did little to improve the team's overall performance.

Darius Miles, acquired from Cleveland in a January deal, joined Zach Randolph to become a potent one-two scoring duo, as the Blazers won 12 of 17 in March and April to get back into the race. However, an overtime loss in Denver, 110–100, with three games remaining, closed the door on any playoff hopes. When the season ended,

(above) Nate McMillan
(opposite) Brandon Roy was the sixth player selected in the 2006 NBA Draft.
(previous spread) Roy stands tall against the Phoenix Suns at Memorial Coliseum.

the only thing left for the Trail Blazers to celebrate was Zach Randolph's selection as the NBA's Most Improved Player. To win that honor, Randolph finished the season as one of only five NBA players to average 20 or more points and 10 or more rebounds a game. The others to do it that season were league MVP candidates Kevin Garnett of Minnesota, Tim Duncan of San Antonio, Shaquille O'Neal of the Los Angeles Lakers, and ex-Blazer Jermaine O'Neal of the Indiana Pacers.

The following season was worse. The Blazers used the 13th pick in the 2004 draft on the highly touted but overmatched New York City high school phenom Sebastian Telfair, a favorite of Blazers general manager John Nash. Assistant general manager Mark Warkentien had urged Nash to take Al Jefferson, who was chosen by Boston two picks later. One could argue that Jefferson, also a high schooler, was just as big a gamble as Telfair, whose greatest claim to fame on draft day was signing a $12 million Adidas sneaker deal and landing on the cover of *Sports Illustrated* at the age of 16. But even if Jefferson was deemed a bad choice on a team that already had the young Zach Randolph as its power forward, Nash had other options: Josh Smith of Atlanta; Jameer Nelson of Orlando; Kevin Martin, who was taken by Sacramento; and Trevor Ariza, a second-round selection by the Knicks.

Yet the hype around Telfair was too tempting for Nash to ignore, given that the Trail Blazers were trying to improve their image and earn some positive national media attention for a change. Telfair could do that. Indeed, not many rookies who had never played a second of college basketball had their own documentary film, *Through the Fire*, broadcast on national television. During his senior year, some of Telfair's high school games, like those of LeBron James a year earlier, were featured presentations on ESPN.

Everybody in marketing wanted a piece of Sebastian Telfair. He was big news in New York—the next big thing, according to his press clips. Accordingly, tickets to Telfair's games at Lincoln High were tougher to get than tickets to the New Jersey Nets. In the end, the Sebastian Telfair story is both classic (the movies *Hoop Dreams*, *He Got Game*, and *Finding Forrester* come to mind) and tragic. He had some good games with the Blazers, and was well liked by the coaching staff and his teammates,

(below) Sebastian Telfair poses for the camera.
(opposite) Zach Randolph attacks the rim.

but contrary to the advanced billing, Sebastian was not the next big thing. As a rookie, he averaged only 6.8 points and 3.3 assists in 68 games, logging about 20 minutes a game as Damon Stoudamire's backup. Nash's other three choices in the 2004 draft were foreigners—Viktor Khryapa and Sergei Monia of Russia and Ha Seung-Jin of South Korea, which inspired one national broadcaster to quip, "Who can say that these names won't be remembered among the Trail Blazer basketball elite? Who can say these names?"

Zach Randolph's game, in 2004–05, held up until he missed the final 27 games with a knee injury that eventually required microfracture surgery. The Blazers won only 5 of those 27 games. Key contributors, such as Randolph, Miles, and Shareef Abdur-Rahim, one of the best Blazer forwards of the mid-2000s, missed a total of 107 games after January 1. The only positive things that emerged from that doomed campaign were a couple of outstanding individual performances—one by Damon Stoudamire, who scored a club-record 54 points on January 14 in a loss at New Orleans (See Appendix C, "The 50-Point Blazer Club"), and the other by Miles, whose 47 points and 12 rebounds on April 19 at Denver were impressive, but not good enough, either, as the Blazers lost their 55th game of the season, 119–115. All those losses, the most in a season in 30 years, cost Cheeks his job.

Portland really bottomed out the next season, even though Paul Allen made one of his most significant personnel moves by hiring Nate McMillan as Portland's next head coach in 2005. McMillan had just capped a five-year run with archrival Seattle by leading the Sonics to the Northwest Division title and a trip to the second round of the NBA playoffs.

While the Blazers endured their worst season (21–61) since 1971–72, dead last in the standings, their only hope for the future focused on the speedy development of key young players: Seattle Prep star Martell Webster, Portland's first pick in the 2005 draft; Jarrett Jack, a skillful playmaker out of Georgia Tech; and guards Steve Blake and Juan Dixon, who led Maryland to the 2002 NCAA Championship. Under McMillan, the five-guard rotation of Dixon, Blake, Telfair, and rookies Webster and Jack, with a combined six years of experience, ranked among the Blazers' top eight scorers. On the positive side, the Blazers unloaded the talented but often disgruntled Ruben Patterson, a move that promised happier days in 2006.

What an understatement that became. In perhaps the most active and successful day of deal making in league history, Steve Patterson and Pritchard executed six deals involving six teams, 13 players, and five draft choices, literally building a future playoff contender in a matter of 24 hours. The Blazers started the day with just the fourth pick overall, allocated from the NBA's lottery system, which actually was the worst selection Portland could have earned, odds-wise, from its last-place finish in 2005–06. In their first trade with Chicago, the Blazers sent Viktor Khryapa and Portland's fourth pick, Tyrus Thomas of LSU, to Chicago for the Bulls' second pick, LaMarcus Aldridge of Texas.

(top and above) Player personnel director Kevin Pritchard was named interim head coach after Maurice Cheeks's departure during the 2004–05 season. *(opposite, left to right)* John Nash, Nate McMillan, Paul Allen, and Steve Patterson at a July 2005 press conference to announce McMillan's hiring as Portland's 12th head coach.

"IN THE RING
      OR OUT,
THERE IS NOTHING
   WRONG WITH
GOING DOWN.
   IT'S STAYING
DOWN THAT'S
   WRONG."

—MUHAMMAD ALI

Brandon Roy and LaMarcus Aldridge sign autographs for a few lucky fans.

The Blazers then shipped Sebastian Telfair to the Boston Celtics, along with veteran center Theo Ratliff and a 2008 second-round pick, in exchange for Boston's seventh pick, Randy Foye, plus Raef LaFrentz and Dan Dickau. Almost immediately, Portland handed over Foye to Minnesota for the rights to Brandon Roy.

Later in the day, Portland purchased the rights to the Spanish guard Sergio Rodriguez from Phoenix. In all, the Trail Blazers pulled the trigger on a draft-day-record six trades. So, summing up, the Blazers got the 6-foot-6 Roy of Washington and the 6-foot-11 Aldridge as the cornerstones of a new Blazer era, plus clever playmaker Rodriguez and three second-round picks—all in a day's work.

These acquisitions translated nicely to an 11-game improvement in the standings, as Roy averaged 16.8 points per game and was a near-unanimous choice for NBA Rookie of the Year. McMillan, nevertheless, was displeased, as Portland lost six of its last seven games, the one shining light being the play of four-year veteran Travis

(left) Brandon Roy drives the lane against Kevin Garnett and the Minnesota Timberwolves.
(below, left to right*)* In the huddle with Maurice Lucas, Darius Miles, Raef LaFrentz, and LaMarcus Aldridge

Outlaw, who scored back-to-back career highs of 26 and 36 points in the final games of the season. Drafted out of high school in 2003, and seemingly lost among the great Douglas firs of the Pacific Northwest, Outlaw was finally beginning to show that he had game and was ready to take part in a Blazer revival. Even though the Blazers' record was full of hope, there were still a few glitches to iron out: (1) Roy and veteran Zach Randolph seemed to clash over who would be the team leader, and (2) despite a preseason trade to bring Milwaukee center Jamaal Magloire to Portland, the Blazers were in need of an intimidating center if they were to contend for a future NBA championship.

Pritchard's tenure as general manager started with a lucky bounce of the ball. May 22, 2007, was the day that most Blazer fans started to believe in miracles. Despite having just a 5.3 percent chance that those NBA Draft lottery balls would fall in the right order to award Portland the No. 1 pick, Brandon Roy was there in the WaMu Theater at Madison Square Garden to claim the prize—7-foot Greg Oden of Ohio

State, thought by most talent scouts to be that once-in-a-generation big man that most serious NBA title contenders need to get it done.

Drama replaced euphoria for a while as a case could be made just as easily that Kevin Durant of Texas, the high-scoring forward that many scouts felt would make it some day to the NBA Hall of Fame, should be the Blazers' choice. But most Trail Blazer fans, in a newspaper poll—and, indeed, a vast majority of the NBA's scouts and general managers—argued that you simply couldn't pass up a generational big man, even if it would take him a little time to fully realize his potential.

So when the Blazers introduced Oden to Oregon in the early summer of 2007, more than 10,000 Blazer fans showed up in Pioneer Square to shout their approval for the first player taken in the NBA Draft. But the excitement didn't last long. Following a mediocre summer camp, Oden suffered a major knee injury and in September had microfracture surgery on his right knee that forced him to miss his first season. Meanwhile, Durant flourished in Seattle, winning Rookie of the Year honors.

The Blazers, without Oden, did OK, too. They didn't make the playoffs, but they did improve their record by nine more games, breaking even at 41–41. Part of the improvement had to do with Pritchard's other moves on June 28, the 2007 draft day. As if not satisfied that the team had stolen Oden from the law of averages, Pritchard traded Zach Randolph and guards Freddy Jones and Dan Dickau to the Knicks for forward Channing Frye and guard Steve Francis, eventually waiving Francis, who was past his prime.

(Note: Dickau, who grew up in the Portland area, goes down in Trail Blazer history as the only player to have been acquired twice in trades, in 2004 from Atlanta and in 2006 from Boston, and traded away twice, in 2004 to Golden State, and in 2007 to New York.)

The Blazers then acquired guard James Jones and the draft rights to the Spanish star Rudy Fernandez from Phoenix. Despite Oden's absence, all these new players made the Blazers not only better but also more interesting. Roy continued his rise to

(above) Leading up to the 2007 NBA Draft, a Portland billboard asks the all-important question: Should the Trail Blazers take Greg Oden or Kevin Durant with the first pick?
(opposite top) Greg Oden (right) shakes hands with NBA Commissioner David Stern (left) after being selected first during the 2007 NBA Draft at the WaMu Theatre at Madison Square Garden.
(opposite middle) Greg Oden's contagious smile.
(opposite bottom) Greg Oden faces the media crush prior to the 2007 NBA Draft in New York.

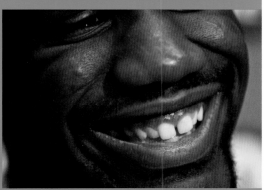

stardom, making the All-Star team for the second time with a 19.1 scoring average, while Aldridge continued his growth at power forward, garnering 17.8 points and 7.6 rebounds per game. But the biggest surprise was the continued improvement and growing confidence of Travis Outlaw, who was becoming a steady fourth-quarter go-to guy when Roy and Aldridge were scrambling against double teams.

If there was a defining moment this decade, when the young Trail Blazers discovered themselves and their potential as a future contender in the NBA, it was December 3, 2007, in an unexpected, but sorely needed, 106–105 road win at Memphis.

The victory was the Blazers' first on the road that season, ending a 9-game road losing streak, and it came after a disheartening stretch in which they had lost 4 games in a row and 9 out of 10.

Most fans will remember it as the game in which Travis Outlaw, in his fifth season with the Blazers and still playing like a raw rookie at times, grew up—showing signs that he could deliver that fourth-quarter dagger.

Outlaw scored the team's final 7 points, including a wild, floating bank shot at the buzzer to win the game. His heroics instilled a new sense of confidence in the players. They swarmed him as if he had just hit the shot that clinched a playoff berth.

This win was memorable, too, because it launched a 13-game Portland winning streak, making the Blazers—the also-rans of the previous three seasons—the talk of the league.

"The one thing I didn't see from our guys tonight was a sense that they couldn't win," coach Nate McMillan said afterward. "The last few games that we've played, sometimes there was doubt on our faces. But tonight, they had a little swagger to them and they looked like they believed in themselves."

Greg Oden, the first player taken in the 2007 NBA Draft, is greeted by an estimated 10,000 fans gathered at Pioneer Courthouse Square on June 29, 2007.

The victory, however, didn't come easy for the Blazers (6–12). Rudy Gay followed a miss by Juan Carlos Navarro with a put-back layup to give Memphis the lead, 105–104, with just 2.8 seconds left.

The Blazers called a timeout, and McMillan drew up a play for reigning Rookie of the Year Brandon Roy, who so often in his young career has been clutch for the Blazers in the fourth quarter of tight games.

But the Grizzlies blanketed Roy with defenders, so James Jones, the inbounds passer, scanned the floor for another teammate and saw Outlaw break free near midcourt.

Outlaw collected the pass and drove hard to the basket, and with Roy screaming, "Shoot it!" over and over, Outlaw pulled up from six feet and released a runner at the last possible moment. The shot bounced in off the backboard, touching off a rowdy celebration near the Blazers' bench as players hugged one another.

"I was hoping to get fouled, but they didn't call anything and [the ball] went in, and I was like, 'Ohhh.' It was nice," Outlaw told the *Oregonian* afterward.

"Travis was hungry and he wanted the ball," Roy said in describing the winning play. "I thought he was going to do a one-dribble pullup, like he normally does. But he took it all the way to the basket. I'm just amazed at how patient he was. But he had it all the way."

Down the stretch, Outlaw made the difference: He sank a nine-foot jumper with 56.2 seconds left and swished a clutch 3-pointer with 15.9 seconds left to set up his season-changing game winner. He finished with 21 points and 7 rebounds. The Blazers also saw a return-to-form performance from Roy, who ended a week-and-a-half malaise by scoring a team-high 26 points and collecting 9 rebounds and 7 assists. LaMarcus Aldridge added 23 points, and Jones scored a season-high 16 points, thanks to four 3-pointers.

This game was a turning point in Outlaw's career. No longer was he shy about taking clutch shots, waiting for his best friend Roy to win games. Clearly this was the day he grew to NBA manhood—and he did it in front of 12 family members, including his father and grandfather, who were watching from the front row.

"SOMETIMES WE STARE SO LONG AT A DOOR THAT IS CLOSING THAT WE SEE TOO LATE THE ONE THAT IS **OPEN**."

—ALEXANDER GRAHAM BELL

(below) Trail Blazers president Larry Miller (left) and president emeritus Harry Glickman (right) visit Mark Morris High School in Longview, Washington, the site of Portland's first-ever preseason game. A delegation of Blazers past and present visited the school during the 2009–10 season commemorating the 40-year anniversary.
(opposite) Brandon Roy makes his presence known at the 2009 All-Star Game.

The next two seasons continued to cast the Blazers, the youngest team in the NBA, as a team on a mission to make something of themselves after years of undisciplined appetites for individual glory.

The Blazer organization, led by president Larry Miller and COO Sarah Mensah, continued to look for opportunities to inspire and reinvigorate Blazer fans to believe in the brand again, "Rise With Us," as the team's slogan says. Once that was accomplished, they, along with Pritchard and McMillan, looked for smaller ways to make the team better. The 2008 draft was part of that. Once again, as they had done in 2006, the Blazers selected four players that they never kept beyond the first two hours of the draft.

First, they sent Jarrett Jack and forward Josh McRoberts, a Blazer pick in 2007, and the draft rights to Kansas guard Brandon Rush to Indiana for veteran forward Ike Diogu and the rights to Jerryd Bayless of Arizona. Then, after acquiring Darrell Arthur of Kansas and Joey Dorsey of Memphis in the draft, they traded both of them to Houston for the rights to French forward Nicolas Batum. That trade may one day rank as one of Portland's best moves, given Batum's development as a defender and a 3-point shooter. After the 2008 summer league in Las Vegas, in which Batum looked like a lost fawn on a dark

Brandon Roy greets an estimated 10,000 fans gathered at Pioneer Courthouse Square for a rally prior to the start of the 2009 NBA Playoffs.

mountain road, ESPN's John Hollinger concluded in a June 28, 2008, column about the Euro rookie class that Batum simply "can't play."

Not only did Batum surprise Hollinger and many Blazer boosters by making Portland's 12-man roster, but he was the starting small forward in 76 of Portland's 82 games.

The Blazers in 2008–09 brought back memories of the good old "Red Hot and Rollin'" days. With Oden healthy, after missing his entire rookie season with major knee surgery, Portland won 14 of its first 20 games, including six wins in a row at one stretch. Fans also got their first up-close look at Oden, who fulfilled all expectations at the defensive end of the court with his rebounding, shot blocking, and overall intimidation. His 7-foot, 260-pound presence made the Blazer defense formidable. On the other end of the court, Oden remained a work in progress.

Oden did have a breakout game, though it offered a false promise for a breakout season. On January 19 at the Rose Garden, against Milwaukee, Oden scored a career-high 24 points, with a then career-high 15 rebounds as the Blazers routed the Bucks, 102–85. As he meandered off the court, his face set in a perennial solemn stare, a sellout Rose Garden crowd of 20,580 rewarded him with a resounding standing ovation, befitting the monstrous game they had just witnessed.

(below) Travis Outlaw
(opposite) Nicolas Batum

Oden made 9 of 14 shots and 6 of 11 free throws, and added 2 steals and 2 blocked shots. His final stats line was more than double his totals for the previous three games combined (12 points, 7 rebounds). Once again, though, Oden's season was slowed by injury, his learning process interrupted. He played only 61 games, missing two stretches, one due to a bone chip in his left knee and the other due to a foot sprain.

The 2009 Blazers won 10 of their final 11 games, claiming their first appearance in the playoffs since 2003 and their first home-court advantage in the first round of the playoffs in nine years.

But even with Oden back in the lineup and healthy down the stretch, the Blazers, still the youngest team in the NBA, and, as such, reminiscent of the 1977 champion Blazers, showed their youth and inexperience against the Houston Rockets, losing the opener, 108–81, and eventually the series, 4–2.

It was a great season for a lot of Blazers. Brandon Roy made the All-Star team again and twice was named the NBA's Western Conference Player of the Week. Stylish rookie Rudy Fernandez was selected by fans to appear in the league's Slam Dunk contest at the All-Star game, and later was selected to the NBA's All-Rookie second team after setting an NBA rookie record for most 3-pointers in a season (159).

Greg Oden takes in the action at the Trail Blazers 2009–10 training camp at the team's practice facility in Tualatin, Oregon.

LaMarcus Aldridge boosted his scoring average to 18.1 points per game and led the team with 19 double-doubles (points and rebounds).

And Nate McMillan, named Western Conference Coach of the Month for April, led this young team (average age, 23.8 years), to 54 wins, more than any Trail Blazer team in nine years, and a share with Denver of the Northwest Division title.

As for Portland's long-term future, it was clear to most NBA observers that the heavy lifting had been done in the prior drafts, and now it was time for the Blazers to jell, to polish the rough spots, to get healthy, and to grow from the young boys of Portland to the fear-nobody men of the West.

In planning for the 2009 season, Portland hadn't expected to be quite so active as in years before. So on draft day, the Blazers swapped picks with Dallas to draft Spanish forward Victor Claver, planning to leave him playing in Europe for a few years. In the second round, the Blazers acquired the draft rights to forward Jeff Pendergraph from Sacramento in exchange for guard Sergio Rodriguez. With its other two picks in the second round, Portland chose Dante Cunningham of Villanova and Patty Mills, an Australian National Team player who starred at St. Mary's (CA). None of these players were projected to play major minutes, if at all, until the most infectious injury plague in Blazer history virtually took out five of the top eight players in the Blazer rotation—not just for a few days or weeks, but for several months, including both centers, Greg Oden and Joel Przybilla, who were knocked out for the season with knee surgeries. Indeed, the Blazers led the league in players requiring surgery, with eight:

(below) An excited Trail Blazer fan greets the team as they come onto the floor.
(opposite) A young fan gets the proper branding prior to a Blazers game at the Rose Garden.

The Portland French School

FRENCH SCHOOL

Nicolas Batum enjoys a visit with fans at Portland's French School.

Portland forward LaMarcus Aldridge takes it to the hoop against Memphis.

Mills, Batum, Jeff Pendergraph, Outlaw, Oden, Przybilla, Fernandez, and finally Roy. For the year, Portland players, most of them key rotation players, lost 311 games to injuries, second in the NBA to Golden State, but first among playoff teams. While no league records are kept about players lost to injuries for the season, it's quite likely that no other playoff team ever had to overcome such adversity.

This wave of injuries took its toll on McMillan, both emotionally and physically. Perhaps the lowest point of his 21-year career as a player and a coach in the NBA came December 4 at the team's Tualatin practice facility. While he and assistant coach Monty Williams participated in a scrimmage, because the shorthanded Blazers didn't have enough healthy players to play five-on-five, McMillan ruptured his right Achilles tendon and required surgery. The next day, crutches in hand, McMillan watched his team defeat Houston, 90–89, but in the process, the club lost franchise center Greg Oden to a season-ending knee injury, while also learning that night that its best perimeter shooter and hustle leader, Rudy Fernandez, would be sidelined for an extended period of time (19 games) due to a back injury that required surgery.

During a somber postgame press conference, the usually stoic and unflappable McMillan, wearing a boot on his right foot and obviously feeling some physical pain, was as close to tears as the media has ever seen him. "This has gone well past crazy," he said. "It's gotten to the point that I'm afraid when our guys are on the floor. When a guy goes down as often as it is happening to us, it makes you wonder if this is more than just happenstance," he said. Then he added, "Yes, it will be a big challenge to overcome this, but our guys will deal with it."

(opposite) Joel Przybilla and his son greet fans gathered at a 2009 NBA Playoff rally at Pioneer Courthouse Square.
(top) Brandon Roy and his son at a press conference announcing Roy's contract extension.
(bottom) Steve Blake chats with his family while out on the road.

"THE GREATEST DANGER A TEAM FACES ISN'T THAT IT WON'T BECOME SUCCESSFUL, BUT THAT IT WILL, AND THEN CEASE TO IMPROVE."

—MARK SANBORN, LEADERSHIP SPEAKER

The poet's path was indeed the road the 2009–10 Blazers chose to travel; to overcome adversity, the coaches drew out abilities that many of their players didn't know they had. Nicolas Batum, for example, was a great defender but had been a passive offensive player throughout his rookie year. But after returning to the starting lineup, after missing 45 games to preseason shoulder surgery, Batum showed his hidden talents: He scored a career-high 31 points February 27 to lead the visiting Blazers past Minnesota, 110–91. His stats line: 11 of 16 from the floor, 5 of 8 on 3-pointers, 4 of 4 free throws, 7 rebounds, 7 assists, 3 steals, and no turnovers. McMillan and his staff, anchored by lead assistant coach Dean Demopoulos, seized upon the injury crisis as an opportunity for discovery, for utilizing Portland's deep bench, and for redesigning the master plan. As a result, Cunningham, Pendergraph, and even Patty Mills saw some playing time, and Pritchard's two off-season free agent signings, 11-year veteran guard Andre Miller and 16-year veteran forward-center Juwan Howard, were given major minutes. And down the stretch, Portland scored another coup by sending the injured forward Travis Outlaw and guard Steve Blake to the Los Angeles Clippers for 6-foot-11 center Marcus Camby. Camby is one of the league's best rebounders and shot blockers and was the key to Portland's amazing run to the playoffs, including a 30-point, 13-rebound game that helped the Blazers defeat Oklahoma City, 103–95, in the next-to-last game of the season.

Just about everyone, except perhaps some loyal-to-the-bone Blazer fans and the team itself, had written off the 2009–10 Blazers when center Joel Przybilla went down, nine games after Greg Oden did. Yet, game after game, against the West's best, including the Lakers, Denver, Dallas, San Antonio, Oklahoma City, and Phoenix, the Blazers continued to learn how to win games.

Injuries took a toll on the Trail Blazers during the 2009–10 season. Rudy Fernandez *(below)* missed 19 games with an injured back and even head coach Nate McMillan *(bottom)* suffered a torn Achilles tendon. Both injuries required surgery. *(previous spread)* LaMarcus Aldridge (left) and Greg Oden (right) sky for a rebound over Memphis's Marc Gasol.

"SUCCESS IN THE AFFAIRS OF LIFE OFTEN SERVES TO HIDE ONE'S ABILITIES, WHEREAS **ADVERSITY** FREQUENTLY GIVES ONE AN OPPORTUNITY TO DISCOVER THEM."

—HORACE, ROMAN POET

(right) Steve Blake gets nicked.
(below) Greg Oden broke his patella against the Houston Rockets at the Rose Garden.

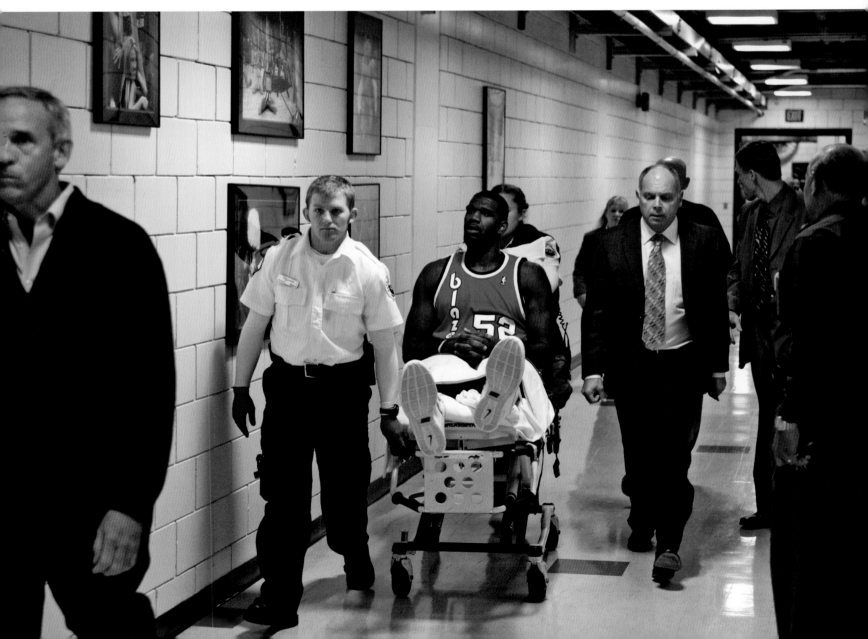

The first of these Trail Blazer missives to the league came December 17 in the form of a Blazers win over Phoenix, 105–102. That was followed by an eye-popping four-game road trip to Florida and Texas. After losing to Orlando, the Blazers won the next three, 102–95 at Miami; 85–81 at Dallas, in which Przybilla suffered a season-ending knee injury; and then the climax—a 98–94 Blazer victory at San Antonio in which Portland played without Oden, Przybilla, and Brandon Roy, but got something very unexpected, a career-high 31 points from Jerryd Bayless and 12 points and 12 rebounds from Juwan Howard.

But the best game of that memorable December stand came on Christmas Day against Denver. Playing out of their minds, as if Santa had bought them a case of Red Bull, the Blazers completed the most unexpected series of wins in franchise history. The topper on the stunning turnaround by the decimated Blazers was a nationally televised 107–96 win over the Nuggets, the team Portland was chasing in the NBA's Northwest Division.

Put another way, there are simply no odds out there to cover what the Blazers did from December 17 to December 25, with road wins over Miami (13–11), Dallas (20–8), and San Antonio (15–10), and home wins against Phoenix (17–8) and Denver (20–9).

Disagree? Then name one other team in the league's 64-year history that lost a starting forward, its only two centers, and its two best scorers off the bench and still managed to win five games in one week against teams with a combined win-loss record at the time of 85–46.

After an epidemic of serious injuries threatened to take their promising season away, the Blazers, led by their All-Star, Brandon Roy, decided in mid-December that

(below) Brandon Roy (left) and LaMarcus Aldridge (right) on the bus from the airport to the team hotel in Los Angeles.
(opposite) LaMarcus Aldridge

enough is enough. Coming into the Christmas Day game, Denver had posted a 16–0 record when leading after three quarters, and the Nuggets took a 76–74 lead into the final 12 minutes, feeling pretty comfortable with it, considering that they had led the Blazers for most of the way. But by now, the Blazers were a completely different team from the one Denver had seen earlier in the year, as Portland played the fourth quarter against the Nuggets like no other NBA team had done.

Led by Roy, the Blazers bashed the heavily favored Nuggets, 33–20, in the fourth quarter, prompting Nugget coach George Karl to say, "They had urgency to their game, and Roy led them at a very high level. We never really got control of his leadership. He had a pretty big stat sheet [41 points, 6 rebounds, and 4 assists], but his drive to take this game away from us was pretty obvious."

The Blazers were an aggressive, fear-no-evil collection of players, some of whom (Juwan Howard, Jerryd Bayless, Jeff Pendergraph) had been primarily DNPs (did not play) on the roster before the injury plague hit. The *Oregonian*'s Trail Blazer beat writer, Jason Quick, captured the essence of the Denver victory when he wrote: "On a day when the NBA trotted out its biggest stars—LeBron James, Kobe Bryant, Dwyane Wade, and Carmelo Anthony—for its Christmas audience to view, one player stole the show: Brandon Roy."

"In one of the most sterling performances of his young career, Roy had a career-high 16 field goals to lead the suddenly streaking Blazers to an important 107–96 win over division rival Denver at the Rose Garden."

Said Roy, "From the opening jump, I was focused, and I wanted that, because this team feeds off me. If they see I'm focused, it makes them more relaxed." It was one of the most well-played games of the season, as Roy, in addition to scoring, drew the brunt of the defensive burden in slowing the league's top scorer, Carmelo Anthony, and limiting him to only 7 points in the final quarter.

Blazer coach Nate McMillan echoed Karl's praise for Roy. "He wanted this game, he really did," McMillan said. "He came out tonight and looked fresh. And we played off him."

"Nice way to spend a Christmas night," added the rookie Pendergraph, whose overall defensive effort against Denver's Kenyon Martin and Chris Anderson was crucial to the win.

Just 14 days later, the Blazers did it again, this time sending the message of redemption south to LaLa Land, home of the world-champion Los Angeles Lakers.

One reason why most Trail Blazer fans consider the Lakers their most feared and hated rival is not one of those Oregon-versus-California jealousy things. Rather, it's because it took the Blazers three seasons and 17 one-sided losses (by an average margin of 17.7 points a game) before they were able to break the Laker hex. Moreover, they did it on the eve of Halloween (October 30, 1973), a fitting time of year for a fledgling franchise, haunted since birth by the seemingly supernatural Lakers, to break the spell. Portland won, 114–112, overcoming an 18-point Laker lead with just 16 minutes left to play.

Fast-forward 37 years to January 8, 2010. This time the Laker hex over the Blazers seemed to be reversed. Even though L.A. had been the vastly superior team over most of the decade, it hadn't been able to beat the Blazers in Portland since February 23, 2005, having to endure eight straight losses.

Nevertheless, the Lakers were still the powerhouse favorite and the NBA defending champion, with a glittery 28–7 record, atop the Western Conference, while the Blazers (22–15) entered the game bruised and battered.

(above) Rudy Fernandez celebrates a 3-pointer.
(opposite) Brandon Roy drives the lane for the game-winning shot versus the Houston Rockets on December 5, 2009.

stom, Andre Miller pours over the
king on the Clippers in Los Angeles.

Playing shorthanded, having lost a starting forward (Nicolas Batum), both centers (Greg Oden and Joel Przybilla), and its top two scorers off the bench (Rudy Fernandez and Travis Outlaw) to various surgeries, Portland did the unthinkable: It ran the Lakers silly.

In one of their more well-rounded and entertaining games of the season, the Blazers controlled the Lakers, 107–98, leading wire to wire, and by as many as 20 points in the fourth quarter, as Brandon Roy played like a serious candidate for league MVP, Martell Webster contributed inspired defense on Laker superstar Kobe Bryant, and Jerryd Bayless's energy off the bench ignited Portland's up-tempo approach.

Roy finished with 32 points, 6 assists, 5 rebounds, and 0 turnovers in 38 minutes. His 32 or more points on 11 or fewer attempts was the most efficient production by an NBA player since March 2008. He matched Bryant in points, but Bryant went 14 for 37 from the field and had 5 turnovers, while Roy went 9 for 11 from the field and 13 of 14 from the free throw line.

"He's a fantastic player," Bryant said of Roy. "One of my favorite players in the league and one of my favorite players to play against. I enjoy watching him. He's very skilled. One of the few players in the NBA who is extremely versatile."

Part of Bryant's shooting struggles were the result of an active defense by Webster, whom McMillan said played his best game as a professional. Webster told the *Oregonian*'s Jason Quick that his defense was about heart and moving his feet.

Bayless also was winged Mercury, alternating determined drives and pinpoint perimeter shots to score 21 points. His drives helped produce 12 free throw attempts and kept the Lakers on their heels.

Blazer coach Nate McMillan had praise for everyone who played, but he reserved his last comments for point guard Andre Miller, who just a day earlier had had a 30-minute shouting match with McMillan in practice over the way he was being used.

"THE BEST THING
ABOUT THE FUTURE
IS THAT IT
COMES ONLY
ONE DAY AT A TIME."

—ABRAHAM LINCOLN

"And my main man Miller," McMillan said, "He played great basketball." Neither McMillan nor Miller would credit their spat, and subsequent reconciliation, as a factor in Miller's effective play (17 points, 7 assists, 4 turnovers), or the team's focused effort. But the airing of pent-up emotions no doubt helped the cause. "It's been a crazy year," said Roy, who made the NBA All-Star team for the third time. "But we are doing a great job of not looking back."

Certainly not looking back to another century—to the year when the Blazers first broke the Laker curse, a time long ago, before Roy, Miller, and the others were even born.

T he 40th Blazer season seemed to have more story lines than a Michael Connelly mystery novel. The injury plague began with the rookies: Patty Mills broke his foot in summer league and underwent surgery; two months later, fellow rookie Jeff Pendergraph had surgery on his left hip. That it took the commitment of the whole team—every one of the 15 signed players the NBA allows on the roster, not just the core veterans—to overcome injuries to Oden, who missed 61 games, Travis Outlaw (55), Przybilla (52), Batum (45), Fernandez (20), and Roy (17) was the major plot line. In all these cases, though, the Blazers proved resilient. When Travis Outlaw broke his foot against the Charlotte Bobcats, the Blazers won by 6. When Greg Oden was lost for the season with a left-knee injury, the Blazers defeated the Houston Rockets at the Rose Garden. When Joel Przybilla was lost for the season with a right-knee injury, the Blazers ended a 10-game losing streak at Dallas and the next day won at San Antonio without Przybilla or Brandon Roy. And in the final week of the season at Los Angeles, Roy went down again with a knee injury with the Lakers cruising in the first half, yet the Blazers rallied behind LaMarcus Aldridge and Martell Webster to defeat L.A., 91–88, and win the season series. The next day, Portland won its season series over Oklahoma City without Roy.

A secondary story was how Juwan Howard discovered the Fountain of Youth; this helped him revive his game to where it was at the beginning of the new millennium, and allowed him to battle the beefier centers of the league on a nightly basis.

(opposite) Martell Webster skies for a block. *(above)* Brandon Roy sits down with Dr. Jack Ramsay for an interview with NBA Radio.

Another subplot was the resurgence of the Blazers potential star of the future, Nicolas Batum, who was a major contributor on both ends of the court as the Blazers won 18 of their last 24 games. Batum's growth as a player in just one season had a lot to do with the lessons he learned from Blazer assistant coach Monty Williams, who worked with the gangly Frenchman one-on-one in practice for much of the season. Williams told the *Oregonian*'s Joe Freeman that he believes Batum has a chance to be "one of the top small forwards in the game in about four or five years." McMillan seconded that notion: He envisions his defensive specialist developing into an impact talent. His high basketball IQ and love of taking on defensive challenges are rare commodities for someone so young.

The addition of Marcus Camby, the missing piece after Oden and Przybilla went down and an inspired defensive presence, gave the Blazers hope that this season the playoffs wouldn't just end up one and done. Indeed, it was the mix of the three veterans,

A Trail Blazers win at the Rose Garden.

Miller, Camby, and Howard, with the Blazer youth movement that began in 2006 that allowed the Blazers to dominate nonplayoff teams 15–1 since February 1.

And, finally, the multiple game-saving clutch plays of guards Brandon Roy and Andre Miller, both of whom learned how to play with, and off of, each other, was another developing story that began in controversy (they both needed and wanted the ball when the Blazers needed a score the most). The two of them carried the team at times, won many games by the force of their very strong wills, and, in the end, developed a relationship that blossomed from rivalry to respect.

For the Blazers, returning to the NBA playoffs for the second straight year and for the 28th time in the franchise's colorful 40-year history is a return to a special place, where Harry Glickman, Stu Inman, Jack Ramsay, Rick Adelman, Geoff Petrie, Bucky Buckwalter, Bill Walton, Clyde Drexler, and many other trailblazing heroes of the past always longed to be.

That place, of course, is Rip City.

◎

Having led the league in surgeries, the wounded Blazers entered their playoff series against Phoenix as significant underdogs. The long odds were earned the hard way—in the painful days and sleepless nights of physical rehab.

The injury jinx wasn't just bad luck—it was a season-long epidemic. In a sports world that honors the resilience of the human spirit, it was to become one of the better stories of grit and determination. And it made Blazer trainer Jay Jensen and his staff, Geoff Clark and Bob Medina, plus team physicians Don Roberts and Tom Reis, candidates for Most Valuable Performer awards.

Phoenix had finished the season as the hottest team in basketball, having won 14 of its final 16 games. The Blazers closed strong, too, but just before the series opener, the team announced All-Star Brandon Roy was to undergo surgery to repair a torn meniscus in his right knee, and was ruled out for the series.

So it was quite a surprise to some when the resurgent Blazers, without their best player, reversed the home-court advantage by stopping the Suns' running game, winning Game 1, 105–100.

(below) Marcus Camby acknowledges Blazers fans at the Rose Garden after being traded to Portland from the LA Clippers for Steve Blake and Travis Outlaw. (opposite) Juwan Howard prior to leaving his hotel room for a game on the road.

"WHAT LIES BEHIND US
AND WHAT LIES
BEFORE US ARE TINY
MATTERS COMPARED
TO WHAT LIES
WITHIN US!"

—RALPH WALDO EMERSON

It was another fourth-quarter rally that clinched the deal as Andre Miller scored 15 points and tied his career playoff high with 31 points overall. Even without Roy, Portland's methodical half-court offense and inside size advantage was a tough match-up for the Suns. Without the ball, and especially when Portland was hitting high-percentage shots, the Suns couldn't initiate their fast break.

The opening-game victory over the Suns gave Blazer fans hope that the team could reach its preseason goal of getting beyond the first round of the playoffs. But everything seemed to break out for the Suns in Game 2. Amar'e Stoudemire was too elusive and quick inside, especially with Steve Nash, one of the best point guards ever at running the inside pick-and-roll, out there taking charge. And when the Blazers double-teamed, Phoenix punished them from 3-point range. Perhaps the most important move of the entire series came when Phoenix coach Alvin Gentry assigned 6-foot-8 veteran Grant Hill to stalk Miller everywhere he went. The strategy rendered Miller harmless on drives to the basket, and Hill's condor-like wingspan closed up many of the passing lanes.

Portland didn't fare much better in Game 3, as the Suns solved the Trail Blazers' half-court defense with Jason Richardson's hot hand. As the Blazers focused on stopping Stoudemire and Nash, Richardson was continuously left open and made eight 3-pointers on his way to 42 points and a 108–89 Suns victory.

(below) Brandon Roy prepares to meet with the media at the Rose Garden and announce that he'll undergo surgery to repair a torn right meniscus prior to the start of the 2010 NBA Playoffs. The gritty Roy returned to action just two weeks after the surgery. *(opposite top)* Andre Miller records an assist. *(opposite bottom,* left to right) LaMarcus Aldridge, Marcus Camby, and Martell Webster celebrate as time runs out. *(previous spread)* Rookie forward Jeff Pendergraph gets his teammates fired up prior to a big game.

Still, Blazer fans had one more dramatic moment, coming in Game 4. That's when Brandon Roy, his team down two games to one and looking bad doing it, did his walk-on-water trick. As the basketball world and modern medicine looked on with both amazement and admiration, Roy showed up for pregame warm-ups in ready to play just eight days after undergoing arthroscopic surgery on his right knee. While LaMarcus Aldridge led the team with 31 points and 11 rebounds, Roy's return provided the inspiration and hope that fueled the Blazers to a 96–87 win, tying the series at 2–2.

Unfortunately, the inspirational lift that Roy gave the Blazers in Game 4 was absent in Games 5 and 6, as Phoenix ended the Blazers' unexpected playoff run.

The series proved to be a burnout for the Blazers and their fans, but the same couldn't be said for the season. In many ways, it showed the 2009–10 Trail Blazers to be mentally tougher than Blazer teams of the past. They played through misery and came out the better for it. And the scramble to fill positions created opportunities that might not otherwise have existed.

Had Oden and Przybilla not gone down, for instance, fans never would have seen what the seemingly ageless Juwan Howard could do with extended minutes. Nor would Portland have made the deal for Marcus Camby, who was re-signed by the team. Now, along with Oden and Przybilla, this gives the team three legitimate centers. And if Nicolas Batum and Rudy Fernandez had not been injured, McMillan would never have given valuable playing time and experience to rookies Dante Cunningham, Jeff Pendergraph, and Patty Mills.

all year long. With everything that they had to go through, all the injuries, we're not making excuses, but they had to fight through a lot, and we had guys to step up and play and be productive."

The Blazers of 2010 proved they had the talent to compete against the NBA's best; they proved they had the inner strength to overcome adversity; they proved that they had the stuff of champions.

The franchise was 40 years old and proud of it. Their window of opportunity to do something grand seemed as wide open as it had ever been. Decade number five is as bright and full of hope as any other time in Trail Blazer history.

"Can't wait," said Brandon Roy.

(top) Rudy Fernandez shoots from downtown.
(bottom) LaMarcus Aldridge (right) looks to reject Suns guard Steve Nash.
(opposite) Brandon Roy

A disappointed Brandon Roy and LaMarcus Aldridge head for the locker room after falling to the Phoenix Suns, 4–2, in the first round of the 2010 NBA Playoffs.

ROY WONDER

BY JASON QUICK

Brandon Roy doesn't like to putblicize it, but he's claustrophobic. He hates tight spots. Elevators? "I won't get on a crowded elevator. I will take it by myself, or with one other person," Roy says. "Otherwise, I'll wait for the next one."

A sleeping bag? "*Nooo* way," the Trail Blazer star says.

Small airplane? "Un-uh," he says, shaking his head.

Even in small rooms, Roy gets queasy. "If I'm in the doctor's office, especially one that doesn't have windows, I'll ask for the door to be left open," Roy says.

But put Roy in a tight spot in a Blazers game—the clock winding down, the Blazers needing a basket, 20,000 fans in the Rose Garden watching his every move—and the 6-foot-6 guard is perfectly at ease.

In fact, those tight spots have become part of his growing legacy as an all-time Blazer great. In his first four seasons with the Blazers, Roy has either won a game or sent it to overtime 38 times in the game's final 35 seconds, sometimes shooting, sometimes with a pass, sometimes with a defensive play, but all his saves have combined to secure his place as one of Portland's all-time clutch players.

"When the game is getting close, and there's pressure, that's a different type of tight spot," Roy said. "There's no other place I'd rather be." And to think that his introduction as the Blazers' closer came by accident.

It was his rookie season, in his 14th game, when the Blazers needed a basket at the end of a game at Sacramento. Coach Nate McMillan diagrammed a play for then Blazers star Zach Randolph.

But the play broke down before the ball was even inbounded, and Roy flashed to the top of the 3-point circle. With the clock winding down, Roy created his own shot, a fade-away 15-footer from the left side.

Swish. Overtime.

The Blazers went on to beat the Kings, and in the process, a star was born. Soon, Roy was the player McMillan went to late in games, particularly when one shot was the difference between winning or losing.

"If you just go back to all his games, and all his last-second shots, each one made him a bigger star for us," McMillan says. "He was becoming not only an All-Star right before our eyes, but also a guy who made us feel like he could take us to where we want to go. Because these were game-winning plays. And then he would do it again. Do it again. Do it again. Do it again. Do it again. Do it again . . ."

But Roy admits nothing will ever top that one November night in 2008 when, in front of a national television audience, he hit a shot that could very well be the greatest in Blazers history. It came in overtime. Against Houston. And as McMillan would say later, it came "from out of the clouds" in the Rose Garden.

With 0.8 seconds left in overtime, and the Blazers trailing, 99–98, Roy took an inbounds pass from Steve Blake, turned around, and launched a high-arcing 31-footer.

"It felt like I was shooting it at the practice facility, with nobody there. No pressure," Roy says. "Because there was only 0.8 left, I didn't think I was going to make it."

When he let go of the shot, he fell backward to the floor, landing out of bounds and against the scorer's table. "I threw it up, and I couldn't see the rim, because Yao Ming was standing in front of me," Roy says. "But I was to the side of him a little, and all I could see was the bottom of the net. When I saw that ball go through the net, I was on top of the world. It was a once-in-a-lifetime moment."

Roy said he nearly didn't sleep the rest of that night. "I went home and rewinded it. Rewinded it. Rewinded it," Roy says, giggling. "Then I would rewind it again. The whole smile on my face."

The funny thing is, Roy was almost the goat. He was only 5 for 17 from the field, and had allowed Houston to take the lead moments earlier when he fouled Ming while the giant center made a baseline jumper.

"Up until that moment, it was probably one of my most frustrating games," Roy says. "Ron Artest took me out of everything. But once I hit it, it felt like I had scored 50."

Actually, at that point, Roy never knew what scoring 50 felt like. But five weeks later he would find out, when he set the Rose Garden scoring record of 52 points against Phoenix. It ranks tied for second in Blazer history.

Roy claims he could feel something special in the air that night, so much so that he had to tell someone. That someone was assistant coach Kaleb Canales. "I remember walking off the court after warm-ups and telling Kaleb that I felt good," Roy says. "My body just felt right. And that gave me a lot of confidence."

That translated into a sensational game, during which Roy hit 14 of 27 shots, five of seven 3-pointers, and 19 of 21 free throws. He also had 6 assists, 5 rebounds, and 0 turnovers in 44 minutes.

"I felt every shot that left my hands was going to go in," Roy says. "It didn't matter if you shrunk that basket, I was going to get it in there. That's the kind of night it was."

Many memorable nights would follow — like in 2009-10, when Roy established a franchise record by scoring 23 or more points in 15 consecutive games. But the night that Roy will never forget happened to come when he was unable to play. It was late January 2010, and it was when Roy first started to understand his place among the Trail Blazer greats.

He was home in Seattle, nursing a right-hamstring injury and unable to attend the Blazers' game in Houston. Watching on television, Roy listened as the Rockets broadcasters spoke of his absence. One of the announcers was former Blazers great Clyde Drexler. Roy remembers Drexler saying that if anybody was going to break his Blazers records, he would want it to be Brandon Roy.

"It caught me off guard," Roy says. "I was like, 'Break his records? The greatest Blazer of all time? Me?' That has never even been a thought of mine. For me, I can't even put that in words. As a kid playing basketball, I never thought I would be considered as a top player in a franchise. *Humble* is not a good-enough word to describe how that made me feel. I would have to look in a dictionary for a word to describe it."

It's easy to see why Drexler had that vision.

Just four years into his career in Portland, Roy is already one of the most decorated players in franchise history. He is one of four Blazers to be named to three All-Star games. One of three to win the NBA's Rookie of the Year. And he was the third fastest to record 5,000 points.

On top of it all, he has been the face of the franchise, serving as the light to lead the team out of its darkest times, when fan disconnect and national ridicule threatened the team's future in Portland.

"When he first came here, we probably needed him more off the floor than we did on the floor—and he knew it," McMillan says. "He allowed the organization to use him in that way. He became the face—this clean-cut guy who can play, who becomes an All-Star—but also, off the floor, people liked him. That doesn't come along very often."

And neither does a player who delivers regularly in the clutch.

Ironically, Roy's penchant for late-game heroics always puts him face-to-face with his greatest fear—tight spots.

On a nightly basis, Roy is in the middle of the media frenzy in the Blazers' locker room. There's not an inch for Roy, or reporters to move in as he is asked to recount the latest game. That's part of the risk, Roy figures, in taking last-second shots and being the franchise player. The reward, he figures, is worth it.

"Hitting the last shot never gets easy, but I never shy away from it," Roy says. "Every time, I get nervous, excited—but it's like you can never make it enough. It's a moment that can never get old. As a player, I would love to win by 20, but if the game is tight, it means I have a chance to have another great moment."

Jason Quick covers the Portland Trail Blazers for the *Oregonian*

APPENDIX A
THE PLAYERS

P ortland's trailblazing journey around the NBA over the past 40 years included 14 All-Stars and three Hall of Famers among the 264 players who dressed for the occasion and came along for the ride.

In the fall of 2009, the *Oregonian*'s Jason Quick appointed a select committee of longtime Trail Blazer observers to pick the 40 best players in Blazers' history. The criteria were vague, although the aim was to pick the 40 best players in team history, not the 40 most popular. Statistics and awards were weighed heavily, as were roles played on winning teams. The eight were selected from the 1976–77 championship team and seven each from Blazer teams that went deep into the playoffs (1990–92 and 1999–2000). Bad character was not held against players, but good character was taken into account. Also, players were judged primarily on their time in a Blazers uniform.

The panel included the *Oregonian*'s current Blazer beat writers Quick and Joe Freeman, former Blazer beat writers Wayne Thompson and Kenny Wheeler, ex-*Oregonian* sports writer Nick Bertram, who defined the term "BlazerMania" in an April 12, 1978 story about fan fever, Trail Blazers archivist Chuck Charnquist, and the legendary radio voice of the Blazers, Bill Schonely.

Following is a list of those players as they were ranked, including a brief profile and the panel's choice of the best game each ever played.

1. CLYDE DREXLER 6-7, guard/forward, Houston; eight-time NBA All-Star; member of the Olympic Dream Team; elected to the Naismith Basketball Hall of Fame. Drexler's No. 22 was retired by the Blazers March 6, 2001. Drexler's best game was January 6, 1989, in Portland's 147–142 double-overtime victory over the Sacramento Kings. Drexler scored a career-high 50 points against the Kings, connecting on 19 of 28 floor shots and 12 of 16 free throws. He added 7 rebounds, 4 assists, and 3 steals to his highlight-film performance. Named in 1996 as one of the top fifty NBA players of all time. Had triple doubles in 21 games as a Blazer, including a game at Milwaukee (January 10, 1986) when he was one assist short of a quadruple-double, (26 points, 11 rebounds, 10 steals, 9 assists). Averaged 20.8 points per game in 12 seasons with the Blazers

2. BILL WALTON 6-11, center, UCLA; two-time NBA All-Star; league MVP, 1977–78; playoff MVP, 1976–77; elected to the Naismith Basketball Hall of Fame. The Blazers retired Walton's No. 32 November 3, 1989. Top rebounder in Trail Blazer history (13.5 per game, 19.1 on a rebound-per-minute basis). Walton's best game was June 5, 1977, when Portland defeated the Philadelphia 76ers, 109–107, to clinch the 1977 NBA championship. Bill had 20 points, 23 rebounds—including 20 defensive rebounds (a championship finals record that still stands today)—and 8 blocked shots. In his two best seasons with the Blazers (1976–78), he averaged 18.8 points per game in 123 games. Greatest compliment, from Celtics general manager Red Auerbach: "I'd rather have two healthy years out of Bill Walton than a full career from most anybody else I've seen since." His son Luke plays for the Lakers.

3. TERRY PORTER 6-3, guard, Wisconsin–Stevens Point; two-time NBA All-Star; Portland career leader in assists (5,319) and 3-pointers made (773); winner of J. Walter Kennedy Citizenship Award, May 3, 1993. The Blazers retired his No. 30 in December 2008. Porter's best game was December 1, 1990, at Seattle as the Blazers defeated the Sonics, 130–124, in three overtimes. He scored 38 points, but it was his desperation heave, tying the score at the buzzer of the first overtime, that will be remembered. Porter made similar game-saving or game-winning treys on at least six other occasions during his 758-game Blazer career. He is considered by many to be the greatest clutch shooter in Blazer history. He was so confident in his ability to make the crucial tying and winning shots that his teammates referred to him as Grande Huevos—"Big Eggs"—the Spanish version of Mr. Clutch. On November 14, 1992, in a 130–116 Blazer win over Golden State, Terry sank seven of seven 3-pointers (still a franchise best) en route to a career-high 40 points.

4. GEOFF PETRIE 6-4, guard, Princeton; two-time NBA All-Star; co–NBA Rookie of Year, 1971; one of only eight players in NBA history to score more than 2,000 points in his rookie season, and one of only three guards to do it (Oscar Robertson and Michael Jordan are the others). Petrie's No. 45 was retired October 11, 1981. Petrie had two best games, both in 1973 against Houston (January 20, March 16), when he scored a then franchise-record 51 points. In those two Portland victories, Petrie connected on 38 of 63 field goals (that was before the league adopted the 3-point field goal rule), and 26 of 30 free throws. He scored 40 or more points 12 times, appeared in two NBA All-Star games, and averaged 21.8 points per game in six Blazer seasons—fourth highest in Blazer history.

5. MAURICE LUCAS 6-9, forward, Marquette; three-time NBA All-Star; twice named to the NBA's All-Defensive team; averaged 12.6 rebounds in NBA championship finals win over the 76ers. Lucas's No. 20 was retired November 4, 1988. Luke's best game came February 3, 1977, at Indiana when he scored 35 points and snared 22 rebounds in a 107–98 Blazer victory. His greatest individual performance came January 12, 1979, at Boston when he scored an NBA career-high 46 points, with 17 rebounds, in a 128–125 loss. Lucas's value to the Blazers as both a player and a coach can't be measured by statistics, though they rank him among the top power forwards in Blazer history. He was the intimidating enforcer of the great Bill Walton teams, assuring his teammates that nobody would be messing with them.

6. BRANDON ROY 6-6, guard, Washington; three-time NBA All-Star; 2007 NBA Rookie of Year; second All-NBA Team in 2008–09; 2009 Magic Johnson Award (to a player who combines court excellence with outstanding cooperation with the media). Just finishing his fourth NBA season, Roy has had several outstanding games to consider, including three in which he canned the game-winning shot in the closing seconds. His best one, on December 18, 2008, came in a 124–119 win against Phoenix. He scored a career-high 52 points on 14 of 27 shooting, including 5 of 7 threes, and 19 of 21 free throws. He is as good as Dwyane Wade at wiggling his way, like a 21st-century version of Gayle Sayers, through the defense on drives to the hoop. He seems to be stronger with his off-hand (the left) than his right on finishes and has an above-average vertical leap.

7. BUCK WILLIAMS 6-8, forward, Maryland; NBA All-Defensive team three times; became only the eighth player in NBA history to collect 16,000 points and 12,000 rebounds. Member of 1980 U.S. Olympic team. He led the NBA in field goal percentage (60.2 percent) in 1992. Best game: January 16, 1991, 24 points, 13 rebounds in 120–115 win over Denver. The missing piece and key to Blazers' NBA title finals runs in 1990, 1992. Without him, the 1990–92 Blazers would never have made it to the finals twice.

8. JEROME KERSEY 6-7, forward, Longwood College Virginia; Blazer leader in floor burns per minutes played; second in Blazer career games played and rebounds, third in

free throws made, and fourth in scoring. Kersey won a slam-dunk contest (summer 1986) over Billy Ray Bates, Spud Webb, Clyde Drexler. Best game: May 5, 1990, 25 points, 16 rebounds in a 109–102 playoff win over San Antonio. Never gave up on a loose ball. One of the most popular Blazers, whose standing vertical jump was not only among the highest in the league, but also the quickest from floor to peak.

9. CLIFF ROBINSON 6-10, forward, Connecticut; holds Blazer record for consecutive games played (461); one of five to score 10,000 or more points for Blazers; NBA All-Star in 1994; Sixth Man of the Year (1992–93). He is among the best defensive small forwards of his era (1989–2007); seventh all-time in NBA games played (1,380). Uncle Cliffy's best game as a Blazer: 41 points in a win over Minnesota on January 7, 1996. Scored 50 points for Phoenix at age 33. The NBA ranks him 28th all-time in terms of 3-pointers made (1,253).

10. JIM PAXSON 6-6, guard, Dayton; two-time NBA All-Star. One of four Blazers to score more than 10,000 points and 2,000 assists; fourth in the NBA in free throw shooting (88.9 percent) in 1985–86; team captain (1982–88). He is among the best in the league at moving without the ball. Best game: scored 40 points in Blazers' win over Houston, 121–117; three-time Blazer scoring leader (1981, 1983, 1984). Clutch!

11. MYCHAL THOMPSON 6-10, forward/center, Minnesota; Blazers' all-time leader in defensive rebounds (3,389); a member of the 20/20 club (points, rebounds) four times. All-Rookie team (1978–79). Most career rebounds (4,878 in 551 games) in Blazer history. Best game: April 3, 1981, scored a career-high 40 points in 124–119 overtime win over Kansas City.

12. RASHEED WALLACE 6-11, forward, North Carolina; two-time NBA All-Star, ranked in the top 10 of 14 statistical categories in nine seasons for the Blazers. He made the All-Star rookie team (1996) and is among the best defenders in the NBA. Best game: February 20, 2001, scored career-high 42 points, with 7 rebounds, in a 104–94 Blazer win over Denver.

13. BOB GROSS 6-6, forward, Long Beach State; perhaps the most underrated Blazer of all time. Earned two MVP votes in the 1977 championship series against the 76ers. Led Blazers in scoring, connecting on 22 of 29 shots, in series-clinching wins. MO: fluid motion. The Blazers retired his No.

30 in December 2008. Best Blazer ever at moving without the ball. Great leaper, ambidextrous. Best game: led Blazers in scoring (24 points, 12 of 16 field goals), and ran the great Dr. J. into exhaustion (held Erving to just 1 of 6 in fourth quarter) in 109–107 title clincher on June 5, 1977.

14. SIDNEY WICKS 6-9, forward, UCLA; four-time NBA All-Star; averaged 22.3 points in five Blazer seasons, second best in club history. Rookie of the Year in 1972, though Portland won franchise-low 18 games; one of only nine players in NBA history to score 2,000 points as a rookie. Wicks's stats (seven triple-doubles, six games of 20 points/20 rebounds) rocked Blazer record books, but he was an enigmatic player whose performance fell off with every passing season. Best game: February 26, 1975; 21 points, 27 rebounds in 117–116 overtime win against Lakers. Averaged 22.3 points per game in five seasons, third best for Blazers all-time.

15. LIONEL HOLLINS 6-3, guard, Arizona State; NBA All-Star in 1978; twice voted to the NBA All-Defensive team; averaged 13.8 points per game in five Blazer seasons; physical defender, crafty ball handler, clutch shooter, but streaky. Nickname: Train. The Blazers retired his No. 14 jersey April 18, 2007. NBA All-Rookie team, 1976. Best game: February 22, 1997, scored a career-high 43 points (and a team-record 20 field goals) while wearing a protective fiber-glass mask in a 113–111 win over Boston.

16. KEVIN DUCKWORTH 7-0, center, Eastern Illinois; two-time NBA All-Star (1989, 1991); voted the NBA's Most Improved Player (1987–88); best pick-and-roll center in Blazer history; much maligned due to his massive frame (280 pounds), but quick feet compensated for his bulk. Best game: May 12, 1991: scored a team-high 30 points, with 11 rebounds, in Portland's 104–101 semifinals playoff win at Utah. Very underrated, as big men go. The avid fisherman passed away August 25, 2008, of heart failure at the age of 44.

17. KIKI VANDEWEGHE 6-8, forward, UCLA; prolific scorer in his five seasons with the Blazers (23.5 ppg); scored more points per minutes played than any other Blazer (one point for every 1.46 minutes played). Best game: his debut as a Blazer at Kansas City on October 27, 1984, 47 points on 19 of 23 shooting, Blazers won, 140–119. Repertoire included a jab step (quick move on the baseline) called the Kiki Move. Among the top Blazer career shooters: field goals (52.6 percent), free

"GOOD, BETTER, BEST. NEVER LET IT REST.
UNTIL YOUR GOOD IS BETTER AND YOUR BETTER IS BEST."

—TIM DUNCAN

throws (88.1 percent) and 3-pointers (40.8 percent); all-time leading Blazer scorer—23.5 ppg in five seasons. Father: NBA player (1950–56). Mother: 1952 Miss America. Kiki: gym rat.

18. SCOTTIE PIPPEN 6-8, forward, Central Arkansas; known primarily as Michael Jordan's "Tonto" in Chicago's dynasty years, Pippen had four productive seasons (11.4 ppg) with the Blazers, earning NBA All-Defensive honors in 2000 when the Blazers went 59–23. Best game; February 4, 2003, collected a team-high 25 points and 17 rebounds in a 96–89 win at Orlando; a major factor in Blazers' ten wins in the 2000 Western Conference playoffs, top scorer in four of the wins; became 46th player in NBA history to score 18,000 points, while at Minnesota on March 23, 2002.

19. DAMON STOUDAMIRE 5-10, guard, Arizona; among the top six point guards in Blazer history (Terry Porter, Rod Strickland, Lionel Hollins, Kelvin Ransey, and Andre Miller are the others). He holds the team record for most points in a game (54). Second among Blazers in 3-pointers made (717). Had three triple-doubles during his eight Portland seasons. Best game: January 14, 2005, at New Orleans. Damon tied then franchise records for field goals made (20), points in a half (30), and 3-pointers made (8) in his 54-point game. Mighty Mouse led Blazers three times in foul shooting.

20. ARVYDAS SABONIS 7-3, center, Lithuania; drafted by the Blazers in 1986, joined them nine years later at age 31. Still, he made the All-Rookie team. One of the most versatile big men ever to play the game—great passer, armed with a skyhook reminiscent of Kareem Abdul-Jabbar's. Sabas played eight productive seasons for the Blazers, who were 382–242 during that stretch, making the playoffs every year. Best game: February 25, 1998, as he joined the NBA's 20/20 club with 21 points and 20 rebounds in a 106–101 win over Michael Jordan's Bulls. He called it his most memorable NBA game.

21. ZACH RANDOLPH 6-9, forward, Michigan State; the NBA's Most Improved Player (2004). Selected in the 2000 draft for his rebounding ability (top rebounder in Big Ten history on rebounds-per-minute basis). Z-Bo has great hands, great instincts, great touch around the basket. Top Blazer scorer, rebounder for four seasons (2004–07), a 20/10 guy (20-plus points and 10-plus rebounds a game). Best game: December 18, 2003, 29 points, 20 rebounds in a win

over Phoenix. Career-high 43 points, 17 rebounds, against Memphis March 29, 2007, a beast on the offensive glass.

22. CALVIN NATT 6-6, forward, NE Louisiana; The Blazers acquired him from New Jersey. NBA All-Rookie team (1979–80), with 20.4 ppg average (22.7 ppg with the Blazers); a 17.2 ppg scorer in five Blazer seasons. Good shooter from short range, outstanding post-up game. Led the Blazers (1981–84) in field goal percentages with 57.6, 54.3, and 58.3. Best game: February 23, 1980, scored career-high 39 points in the Blazers' 130–107 win at Detroit. Averaged 17.2 points per game in five seasons with the Blazers. Now a minister, Natt owns a funeral home in Denver.

23. ROD STRICKLAND 6-3, guard, DePaul; made the NBA's top-10 list in assists three times (1993–96); twice dished out team-record 20 assists in a game; led the team with 7.2, 9.0, 8.8, and 9.6 assists per game for four seasons. Among the top point guards in Blazer history—and perhaps the best distributor; recorded two triple-doubles November 22, 1992, and February 15, 1995. Best game: his 18 points, 20 assists, and 8 rebounds on April 5, 1994, helped clinch a playoff berth. Possessed remarkable body control and sleight-of-hand ball-handling skills; a master of the drive-and-dish.

24. BRIAN GRANT 6-9, forward, Xavier; nicknamed Rasta Monsta for his ferocious play and dreadlocked 'do; the enforcer of the 1997–2000 Blazers; gave Karl Malone fits in Portland's 4–1 semifinals series win over the Jazz. Reliable jump shooter, very popular with fans. One of three Blazers (Terry Porter and Chris Dudley are the others) to win the J. Walter Kennedy Citizenship Award for public service to the community. Best game: April 3, 1998, registered 20 points, 20 rebounds, in the Blazers' 109–102 win over Dallas.

25. LLOYD NEAL 6-7, forward/center, Tennessee State; third-round draft pick; Neal was asked to play center against some of the NBA's giants; this test paid off later as Neal was a vital reserve in Portland's NBA championship run; runner-up to Bob McAdoo for '72 Rookie of the Year. His No. 36 was retired March 24, 1979. Nicknamed Bottom for his wide exterior and his birthplace (Talbottom, Georgia), Neal was the MVP of dirty work in Portland's early years and a reliable scorer off the bench in later years. Best game: 33 points, 13 rebounds, on February 9, 1973, in a win over the 76ers; retired after seven seasons due to injuries.

26. DAVE TWARDZIK 6-1, guard, Old Dominion; shot 61.2 percent from the field during Portland's championship season, an all-time Blazer record for a starting player. Twardzik's No. 13 was retired October 11, 1981. Called Pinball for the way he bounced his body off opponents on his way to the hoop. Best game: on March 5, 1976, he scored a career-high 28 points in a 134–104 romp over Seattle. It started a string of 34 consecutive regular-season victories at home. Very-high-IQ player. Also called Elmer Fudd for his facial resemblance to the Looney Tunes cartoon character.

27. LARRY STEELE 6-5, guard/forward, Kentucky; came within one assist of a rare quadruple-double on November 16, 1974, in a win against the Lakers (12 points, 11 rebounds, 10 steals, 9 assists). His No. 15 was retired October 11, 1981. Best game: March 17, 1977, at Golden State; he led the Blazers with 27 points, going 11 for 16 from the floor, in a 115–106 win over the Warriors. Steele is the all-time Blazer leader in fouling out of games (45), and was the NBA's first steals champion with 217 in 1974.

28. LAMARCUS ALDRIDGE 6-11, forward, Texas; named to the T-Mobile All-Rookie First Team in 2007 and was the leading player (18 points, 9 rebounds, 4 assists, 3 steals, 2 blocked shots) for the Sophomore team in the T-Mobile Rookie Challenge game in 2009. Best game: April 3, 2009; it featured two ex-Texas All-Americans, Aldridge and Kevin Durant of Oklahoma City. Aldridge dominated with 35 points, 18 rebounds. Durant was held to 12 in the 107–72 Blazers' romp.

29. KELVIN RANSEY 6-2, guard, Ohio State; named to the NBA's All-Rookie team, 1980–81; made the NBA's top 10 list in assists (1,100) for two seasons (1980–82). Named NBA Player of the Month in March 1981. Traded to Dallas for Wayne Cooper and a first-round choice, who turned out to be Terry Porter. Best game: January 24, 1982, at Boston, 33 points, 10 assists in the Blazers' 123–119 win. He initiated a chapel program for players in Portland that was adopted by many teams league-wide. Blazers' chaplain Al Egg for several seasons had held periodic prayer meetings for any players who wanted them, but Ransey asked Egg to expand the program and hold chapel meetings at every home game. Now, Ransey is an ordained minister in Tupelo, Mississippi.

30. BILLY RAY BATES 6-4, guard, Kentucky State; second Blazer ever to win NBA Player of the Week award (March 1980). Points per minute in 1980–81 rank third all-time in Blazer history. Holds team record for playoff scoring (26.7 ppg). Best game: his first one, in February 1980; Blazer talent scout Stu Inman asked Mike Uporsky, Bates's coach in Bangor, Maine, if Bates was the best player in the Continental League. Uporsky replied, "Stu, Billy Ray may be the best player in your league." A week later, Bates scored 26 points in 20 minutes in his NBA debut, a 110–107 win over Chicago. Bates's vertical leap (44.5 inches) defied gravity; his unofficial measurement is said to be second only to Spud Webb's 46 inches in NBA history.

31. DANNY AINGE 6-5, guard, Brigham Young; the Blazers traded for Ainge in 1990 to be the third guard and sixth man off the bench; he proved to be the 3-point shooter needed to carry the Blazers to a franchise-record 63 wins and the NBA championship finals. Best game: season-high 23 points on 9 of 10 shooting in a 129–100 win at Denver on March 4, 1992; tied the NBA record for most points (9) in playoff overtime in a 115–104 win over Chicago in the championship finals on June 5, 1992.

32. STEVE JOHNSON 6-10, center, Oregon State; NBA All-Star in 1988; thrice led the team in field goal percentage (1986–89) and once in rebounding (7.2, 1986–87); rugged low-post center, finished eighth in the NBA in field goal percentage (55.6). Best game: scored 40 points, with 10 rebounds, at Cleveland, on November 26, 1986; third-leading scorer (16.8) on the Blazers' highest-scoring team (117.9).

33. DARNELL VALENTINE 6-1, guard, Kansas; ranks fifth all-time in team history for playoff assists (161). Like another NBA player, World B. Free, Valentine had tree-trunk-size thighs, but couldn't jump like Free, so Mychal Thompson nicknamed him Ground Jordan. Best game: canned 13 of 15 shots for a career regular-season-high 26 points, with 4 rebounds, 6 assists and 4 steals, in a 110–99 win over the Clippers on February 26, 1985. His playoff high was 29 points in a loss at Phoenix in 1984.

34. JOHNNY DAVIS 6-2, guard, Dayton; Davis was the difference in Portland's only championship. Starting for the first time in Portland's last 11 playoff games (Blazers were 9–2 in those games), Davis used his quickness to harass opposing guards. Bill Walton credits Davis with "turning a very good team into an unbeatable one." Best game: May 22, 1977, after Dave Twardzik sprained his ankle in the playoff series against Denver, Davis got his first playoff start, played 39 minutes, and scored 25 points (10 of 14 shooting) as the Blazers clinched the series.

35. BONZI WELLS 6-5, forward/guard, Ball State; could have been an NBA All-Star, but his head got in the way. Great basketball body, excellent post-up game, but he didn't handle success and fame well; says now he's sorry about his immature behavior; six seasons in Portland "taught me how to grow up, to be a man." A good defender, he twice led the Blazers in steals. Best game: April 23, 2003, when he set a Blazer playoff record with 45 points, connecting on 16 of 24 shots, including five of six 3-pointers and 8 of 11 free throws against Dallas.

36. KENNY CARR 6-7, forward, North Carolina State; one of the unsung Blazer stars of the rebuilding years (1982–87). A hard-nosed defender who took pride in doing all the dirty work in the trenches. One of 10 Blazers to have won a gold medal in the Olympics (1976). Best game: February 28, 1984, scored team-high 26 points, with 13 rebounds, in a 114–106 Blazer win at San Diego. Topped all Blazers in rebounds in the 1986 first-round playoff series against Denver (53 in 4 games, 13.2 average).

37. JOHN JOHNSON 6-7, forward, Iowa; very versatile, could pass, dribble, post-up, shoot with range, defend, and rebound with the best small forwards of the 1970s. Two triple-doubles; 17 points, 10 rebounds, 11 assists at Phoenix on December 13, 1973, and 23-11-11 against Kansas City–Omaha, on April 4, 1975; often showed his ability to lead and control an offense. Best game: scored 29 points, with 11 rebounds, on his 27th birthday, October 18, 1974, as Portland outlasted Cleveland 115–112 in four overtimes.

38. STEVE SMITH 6-8, guard, Michigan State; top perimeter shooter (1999–2000) for 59-win Blazers who went to the Western Conference finals (scored 18.3 ppg in finals series). The second-best free throw shooter (87.0 percent) in Blazer history. U.S. Olympic team gold medalist (2000). Best game: scored 26 points in a 103–93 win over the Los Angeles Lakers in Game 6 of the 2000 Western Conference finals. The second-highest scorer (14.9 ppg) in the 1999–2000 season, behind Rasheed Wallace (16.4 ppg).

39. KERMIT WASHINGTON 6-8, forward, American University; made the NBA All-Star team in 1980. Two-time NBA All-Defensive team (1979–81); twice among the NBA's top 10 in field goal percentage (1979–81: 55.3 and 56.9). Best game: November 17, 1979, scored 27 points, with 17 rebounds and 3 blocked shots, as short-handed Blazers beat Cleveland, 103–96. Fifth-best rebounder (9.5 per game in 173 games) in Blazer history.

40. JIM BARNETT 6-4, guard, Oregon; called Crazy Horse by teammates. Barnett earned the moniker with sometimes weird and wacky behavior in Portland's inaugural season. Barney is forever etched in Blazer history books, having scored the first points in franchise history and later becoming the first Blazer to score 30 and then 40 points in a game. Never met a 25-foot shot he didn't like. He made the long jumper that inspired Blazer radio man Bill Schonely to cry out "Rip City!" which became the club's signature. Best game: scored 38 points in 30 minutes in the 107–102 win over Buffalo on October 31, 1970. "That's the hottest I've ever been," he says.

POSTSCRIPT: Just about every panel that compiles a list ranking the best of the best in sports agrees to disagree with it. Our panel, appointed by the *Oregonian's* Jason Quick, was no different. After much debate, a difficult consensus was reached on our Top 40. Though we didn't pick honorable mentions, there were 10 Blazers who were proposed as worthy of a Top 40 rank but missed the final cut.

Not necessarily in order of their importance, they were center Sam Bowie, who made the list until the very last vote; centers Tom Owens and Joel Przybilla; shooting guards Ron Brewer, Isaiah J. R. Rider, Lafayette "Fat" Lever, and Drazen Petrovic; and point guards Lenny Wilkens, Rick Adelman, and Kenny Anderson.

No panel member mentioned Darius Miles, yet clearly he is one of the most talented Blazers not to appear on the list (47 points at Denver on April 19, 2005). It was generally agreed among panelists that, except for Roy and Aldridge, it was too early to consider current Blazer players for the list, though Nicolas Batum, Andre Miller, Przybilla, Greg Oden, Marcus Camby, and Rudy Fernandez might rate a second look in the next BlazerMania anniversary book.

Like the sandhill crane, a bird taller than your kids, the Blazers migrate to Oregon each and every autumn to grow and mature.

Their flight of passage is all about getting better. And if they do, their time will come.

ALL-TIME TRAIL BLAZERS ROSTERS

1970–71 (29–53)
COACH: ROLLAND TODD
TRAINER: LEO MARTY

Rick Adelman, Jim Barnett, LeRoy Ellis, Claude English, Walt Gilmore, Gary Gregor, Shaler Halimon, Ron Knight, Ed Manning, Stan McKenzie, Dorie Murrey, Geoff Petrie, Dale Schlueter, Bill Stricker

1971–72 (18–64)
COACH: ROLLAND TODD (56 GAMES)
INTERIM COACH: STU INMAN (26 GAMES)
TRAINER: LEO MARTY

Rick Adelman, Gary Gregor, Darral Imhoff, Ron Knight, Jim Marsh, Willie McCarter, Stan McKenzie, Geoff Petrie, Dale Schlueter, Bill Smith, Larry Steele, Sidney Wicks, Charlie Yelverton

1972–73 (21–61)
COACH: JACK MCCLOSKEY
ASSISTANT COACH: NEIL JOHNSTON
TRAINER: LEO MARTY

Rick Adelman, Bob Davis, Charlie Davis, Terry Dischinger, Ollie Johnson, LaRue Martin, Stan McKenzie, Lloyd Neal, Geoff Petrie, Bill Smith, Greg Smith, Larry Steele, Bill Turner, Sidney Wicks, Dave Wohl

1973–74 (27–55)
COACH: JACK MCCLOSKEY
ASSISTANT COACH: NEIL JOHNSTON
TRAINER: LEO MARTY

Charlie Davis, Bernie Fryer, John Johnson, Ollie Johnson, Dennis Layton, LaRue Martin, Lloyd Neal, Geoff Petrie, Rick Roberson, Mark Sibley, Greg Smith, Larry Steele, Bob Verga, Sidney Wicks

1974–75 (38–44)
COACH: LENNY WILKENS
ASSISTANT COACH: TOM MESCHERY
TRAINER: RON CULP

Dan Anderson, Barry Clemens, John Johnson, Phil Lumpkin, LaRue Martin, Lloyd Neal, Geoff Petrie, Greg Smith, Larry Steele, Bill Walton, Sidney Wicks, Lenny Wilkens

1975–76 (37–45)
COACH: LENNY WILKENS
ASSISTANT COACH: TOM MESCHERY
TRAINER: RON CULP

Dan Anderson, Barry Clemens, Bob Gross, Steve Hawes, Lionel Hollins, John Johnson, Steve Jones, Greg Lee, LaRue Martin, Lloyd Neal, Geoff Petrie, Greg Smith, Larry Steele, Bill Walton, Sidney Wicks

1976–77 (49–33, PLAYOFFS 14–5)
COACH: JACK RAMSAY
ASSISTANT COACH: JACK MCKINNEY
TRAINER: RON CULP

Corky Calhoun, Johnny Davis, Herm Gilliam, Bob Gross, Lionel Hollins, Robin Jones, Maurice Lucas, Clyde Mayes, Lloyd Neal, Larry Steele, Dave Twardzik, Wally Walker, Bill Walton

1977–78 (58–24, PLAYOFFS 2–4)
COACH: JACK RAMSAY
ASSISTANT COACH: JACK MCKINNEY
TRAINER: RON CULP

Corky Calhoun, Johnny Davis, Jacky Dorsey, T. R. Dunn, Bob Gross, Lionel Hollins, Maurice Lucas, Lloyd Neal, Willie Norwood, Tom Owens, Dale Schlueter, Larry Steele, Dave Twardzik, Wally Walker, Bill Walton

1978–79 (45–37, PLAYOFFS 1–2)
COACH: JACK RAMSAY
ASSISTANT COACH: JACK MCKINNEY
TRAINER: RON CULP

Kim Anderson, Ron Brewer, T. R. Dunn, Bob Gross, Lionel Hollins, Clemon Johnson, Maurice Lucas, Jim McMillan, Lloyd Neal, Tom Owens, Willie Smith, Larry Steele, Ira Terrell, Mychal Thompson, Dave Twardzik

1979–80 (38–44, PLAYOFFS 1–2)
COACH: JACK RAMSAY
ASSISTANT COACH: BUCKY BUCKWALTER
TRAINER: RON CULP

Billy Ray Bates, Jim Brewer, Ron Brewer, T. R. Dunn, Bob Gross, Lionel Hollins, Abdul Jeelani, Kevin Kunnert, Maurice Lucas, Calvin Natt, Tom Owens, Jim Paxson, Larry Steele, Dave Twardzik, Kermit Washington

1980–81 (45–37, PLAYOFFS 1–2)
COACH: JACK RAMSAY
ASSISTANT COACH: BUCKY BUCKWALTER
TRAINER: RON CULP

Billy Ray Bates, Ron Brewer, Geoff Crompton, Mike Gale, Bob Gross, Roy Hamilton, Michael Harper, Kevin Kunnert, Tom Owens, Calvin Natt, Jim Paxson, Kelvin Ransey, Mychal Thompson, Kermit Washington

1981–82 (42–40)
COACH: JACK RAMSAY
ASSISTANT COACHES: BUCKY BUCKWALTER, JIM LYNAM
TRAINER: RON CULP

Dennis Awtrey, Carl Bailey, Billy Ray Bates, Bob Gross, Petur Gudmundsson, Michael Harper, Kevin Kunnert, Jeff Lamp, Calvin Natt, Jim Paxson, Kelvin Ransey, Mychal Thompson, Darnell Valentine, Peter Verhoeven, Kermit Washington

1982–83 (46–36, PLAYOFFS 3–4)
COACH: JACK RAMSAY
ASSISTANT COACHES: BUCKY BUCKWALTER, JIM LYNAM
TRAINER: RON CULP

Don Buse, Kenny Carr, Wayne Cooper, Jeff Judkins, Jeff Lamp, Lafayette Lever, Hank McDowell, Calvin Natt, Audie Norris, Jim Paxson, Mychal Thompson, Linton Townes, Darnell Valentine, Peter Verhoeven

1983–84 (48–34, PLAYOFFS 2–3)
COACH: JACK RAMSAY
ASSISTANT COACHES: RICK ADELMAN, BUCKY BUCKWALTER
TRAINER: RON CULP

Kenny Carr, Wayne Cooper, Clyde Drexler, Eddie Jordan, Jeff Lamp, Lafayette Lever, Calvin Natt, Audie Norris, Jim Paxson, Tom Piotrowski, Mychal Thompson, Darnell Valentine, Peter Verhoeven

1984–85 (42–40, PLAYOFFS 4–5)
COACH: JACK RAMSAY
ASSISTANT COACHES: RICK ADELMAN, BUCKY BUCKWALTER
TRAINER: RON CULP

Sam Bowie, Kenny Carr, Steve Colter, Clyde Drexler, Jerome Kersey, Audie Norris, Jim Paxson, Tom Scheffler, Bernard Thompson, Mychal Thompson, Darnell Valentine, Kiki Vandeweghe

1985–86 (40–42, PLAYOFFS 1–3)
COACH: JACK RAMSAY
ASSISTANT COACHES: RICK ADELMAN, BUCKY BUCKWALTER
TRAINER: RON CULP

Sam Bowie, Kenny Carr, Steve Colter, Clyde Drexler, Ken Johnson, Caldwell Jones, Jerome Kersey, Brian Martin, Jim Paxson, Terry Porter, Mychal Thompson, Darnell Valentine, Kiki Vandeweghe

1986–87 (49–33, PLAYOFFS 1–3)
COACH: MIKE SCHULER
ASSISTANT COACHES: RICK ADELMAN, JACK SCHALOW
TRAINER: RON CULP

Walter Berry, Joe Binion, Sam Bowie, Kenny Carr, Clyde Drexler, Kevin Duckworth, Chris Engler, Michael Holton, Steve Johnson, Caldwell Jones, Jerome Kersey, Fernando Martin, Jim Paxson, Terry Porter, Ron Rowan, Kiki Vandweghe, Perry Young

1987–88 (53–29, PLAYOFFS 1–3)
COACH: MIKE SCHULER
ASSISTANT COACHES: RICK ADELMAN, JACK SCHALOW
TRAINER: MIKE SHIMENSKY

Richard Anderson, Clyde Drexler, Kevin Duckworth, Kevin Gamble, Michael Holton, Steve Johnson, Caldwell Jones, Charles Jones, Jerome Kersey, Maurice Lucas, Ronnie Murphy, Jim Paxson, Terry Porter, Jerry Sichting, Kiki Vandeweghe, Nikita Wilson

1988–89 (39–43, PLAYOFFS 0–3)
COACH: MIKE SCHULER (47 GAMES)
INTERIM COACH: RICK ADELMAN (35 GAMES)
ASSISTANT COACHES: RICK ADELMAN, MAURICE LUCAS, JACK SCHALOW, JOHN WETZEL
TRAINER: MIKE SHIMENSKY

Richard Anderson, Sam Bowie, Adrian Branch, Mark Bryant, Clyde Drexler, Kevin Duckworth, Rolando Ferreira, Steve Johnson, Caldwell Jones, Jerome Kersey, Craig Neal, Terry Porter, Jerry Sichting, Brook Steppe, Kiki Vandeweghe, Clinton Wheeler, Danny Young

1989–90 (59–23, PLAYOFFS 12–9)
COACH: RICK ADELMAN
ASSISTANT COACHES: JACK SCHALOW, JOHN WETZEL
TRAINER: MIKE SCHIMENSKY

Mark Bryant, Wayne Cooper, Clyde Drexler, Kevin Duckworth, Byron Irvin, Nate Johnston, Jerome Kersey, Drazen Petrovic, Terry Porter, Robert Reid, Cliff Robinson, Buck Williams, Danny Young

1990–91 (63–19, PLAYOFFS 9–7)
COACH: RICK ADELMAN
ASSISTANT COACHES: JACK SCHALOW, JOHN WETZEL
TRAINER: MIKE SCHIMENSKY

Alaa Abdelnaby, Danny Ainge, Mark Bryant, Wayne Cooper, Walter Davis, Clyde Drexler, Kevin Duckworth, Jerome Kersey, Drazen Petrovic, Terry Porter, Cliff Robinson, Buck Williams, Danny Young

1991–92 (57–25, PLAYOFFS 13–8)
COACH: RICK ADELMAN
ASSISTANT COACHES: JACK SCHALOW, JOHN WETZEL
TRAINER: MIKE SHIMENSKY

Alaa Abdelnaby, Danny Ainge, Mark Bryant, Wayne Cooper, Clyde Drexler, Kevin Duckworth, Jerome Kersey, Robert Pack, Terry Porter, Cliff Robinson, Lamont Strothers, Ennis Whatley, Buck Williams, Danny Young

1992–93 (51–31, PLAYOFFS 1–3)
COACH: RICK ADELMAN
ASSISTANT COACHES: JACK SCHALOW,

JOHN WETZEL
TRAINER: MIKE SHIMENSKY

Mark Bryant, Clyde Drexler, Kevin Duckworth, Mario Elie, Dave Johnson, Jerome Kersey, Tracy Murray, Terry Porter, Cliff Robinson, Delaney Rudd, Reggie Smith, Rod Strickland, Buck Williams, Joe Wolf

1993–94 (47–35, PLAYOFFS 1–3)
COACH: RICK ADELMAN
ASSISTANT COACHES: KIP MOTTA, JACK SCHALOW, JOHN WETZEL
TRAINER: MIKE SHIMENSKY

Mark Bryant, Clyde Drexler, Chris Dudley, Harvey Grant, Jaren Jackson, Jerome Kersey, Tracy Murray, Terry Porter, Cliff Robinson, James Robinson, Reggie Smith, Rod Strickland, Kevin Thompson, Buck Williams

1994–95 (44–38, PLAYOFFS 0–3)
COACH: P. J. CARLESIMO
ASSISTANT COACHES: RICK CARLISLE, JOHNNY DAVIS, DICK HARTER
TRAINER: JAY JENSEN

Mark Bryant, Clyde Drexler, Chris Dudley, James Edwards, Harvey Grant, Steve Henson, Jerome Kersey, Negele Knight, Aaron McKie, Tracy Murray, Terry Porter, Cliff Robinson, James Robinson, Rod Strickland, Otis Thorpe, Buck Williams

1995–96 (44–38, PLAYOFFS 2–3)
COACH: P. J. CARLESIMO
ASSISTANT COACHES: RICK CARLISLE, JOHNNY DAVIS, DICK HARTER
TRAINER: JAY JENSEN

Randolph Childress, Anthony Cook, Chris Dudley, Harvey Grant, Aaron McKie, Cliff Robinson, James Robinson, Rumeal Robinson, Arvydas Sabonis, Reggie Slater, Elmore Spencer, Rod Strickland, Gary Trent, Buck Williams, Dontonio Wingfield

1996–97 (49–33, PLAYOFFS 1–3)
COACH: P. J. CARLESIMO
ASSISTANT COACHES: RICK CARLISLE, DICK HARTER, ELSTON TURNER
TRAINER: JAY JENSEN

Kenny Anderson, Stacey Augmon, Marcus Brown, Mitchell Butler, Randolph Childress, Aleksandar Djordjevic, Chris Dudley, Reggie Jordan, Aaron McKie, Ruben Nembhard, Jermaine O'Neal, Isaiah Rider, Cliff Robinson, Rumeal Robinson, Arvydas Sabonis, Gary Trent, Rasheed Wallace, Ennis Whatley, Dontonio Wingfield

1997–98 (46–36, PLAYOFFS 1–3)
COACH: MIKE DUNLEAVY
ASSISTANT COACHES: TONY BROWN, JIM EYEN, BILL MUSSELMAN, ELSTON TURNER
TRAINER: JAY JENSEN

Kenny Anderson, Vincent Askew, Stacey Augmon, Rick Brunson, Kelvin Cato, John

Crotty, Brian Grant, Gary Grant, Sean Higgins, Alton Lister, Jermaine O'Neal, Isaiah J. R. Rider, Carlos Rogers, Arvydas Sabonis, Damon Stoudamire, Gary Trent, Rasheed Wallace, Alvin Williams, Walt Williams, Dontonio Wingfield

1998–99 (35–25, PLAYOFFS 7–6)
COACH: MIKE DUNLEAVY
ASSISTANT COACHES: TONY BROWN, JIM EYEN, TIM GRGURICH, BILL MUSSELMAN, ELSTON TURNER
TRAINER: JAY JENSEN

Greg Anthony, Stacey Augmon, Kelvin Cato, John Crotty, Brian Grant, Gary Grant, Jim Jackson, Jermaine O'Neal, Isaiah J. R. Rider, Carlos Rogers, Arvydas Sabonis, Brian Shaw, Damon Stoudamire, Rasheed Wallace, Bonzi Wells, Walt Williams

1999–2000 (59–23, PLAYOFFS 10–6)
COACH: MIKE DUNLEAVY
ASSISTANT COACHES: TONY BROWN, JIM EYEN, TIM GRGURICH, BILL MUSSELMAN, ELSTON TURNER
TRAINER: JAY JENSEN

Greg Anthony, Stacey Augmon, Brian Grant, Gary Grant, Antonio Harvey, Joe Kleine, Jermaine O'Neal, Scottie Pippen, Arvydas Sabonis, Detlef Schrempf, Steve Smith, Damon Stoudamire, Rasheed Wallace, Bonzi Wells

(above) Only the fourth athletic trainer in Trail Blazers history, Jay Jensen celebrated his 16th season with the club in 2009–2010.

2000–01 (50–32, PLAYOFFS 0–3)
COACH: MIKE DUNLEAVY
ASSISTANT COACHES: TONY BROWN, MIKE D'ANTONI, JIM EYEN, TIM GRGURICH, NEAL MEYER
TRAINER: JAY JENSEN

Greg Anthony, Stacey Augmon, Erick Barkley, Dale Davis, Gary Grant, Antonio Harvey, Shawn Kemp, Will Perdue, Scottie Pippen, Arvydas Sabonis, Detlef Schrempf, Steve Smith, Damon Stoudamire, Rod Strickland, Rasheed Wallace, Bonzi Wells

2001–02 (49–33, PLAYOFFS 0–3)
COACH: MAURICE CHEEKS
ASSISTANT COACHES: HERB BROWN, CALDWELL JONES, JIM LYNAM, DAN PANAGGIO
TRAINER: JAY JENSEN

Derek Anderson, Erick Barkley, Ruben Boumtje-Boumtje, Rick Brunson, Mitchell Butler, Dale Davis, Chris Dudley, Shawn Kemp, Steve Kerr, Ruben Patterson, Scottie Pippen, Zach Randolph, Damon Stoudamire, Rasheed Wallace, Bonzi Wells

2002–03 (50–32, PLAYOFFS 3–4)
COACH: MAURICE CHEEKS
ASSISTANT COACHES: HERB BROWN, GARY GRANT, JIM LYNAM, DAN PANAGGIO
TRAINER: JAY JENSEN

Derek Anderson, Ruben Boumtje-Boumtje, Antonio Daniels, Dale Davis, Chris Dudley, Jeff McInnis, Ruben Patterson, Scottie Pippen, Zach Randolph, Arvydas Sabonis, Charles Smith, Damon Stoudamire, Rasheed Wallace, Bonzi Wells, Qyntel Woods

2003–04 (41–41)
COACH: MAURICE CHEEKS
ASSISTANT COACHES: JIM LYNAM, JOHN LOYER, DAN PANAGGIO, BERNARD SMITH
TRAINER: JAY JENSEN

Shareef Abdur-Rahim, Derek Anderson, Ruben Boumtje-Boumtje, Matt Carroll, Omar Cook, Dale Davis, Dan Dickau, Kaniel Dickens, Desmond Ferguson, Eddie Gill, Jeff McInnis, Tracy Murray, Travis Outlaw, Ruben Patterson, Wesley Person, Zach Randolph, Theo Ratliff, Vladimir Stephania, Damon Stoudamire, Slavko Vranes, Rasheed Wallace, Bonzi Wells, Qyntel Woods

2004–05 (27–55)
COACH: MAURICE CHEEKS (55 GAMES)
INTERIM COACH: KEVIN PRITCHARD (27 GAMES)
ASSISTANT COACHES: TIM GRGURICH, JIM LYNAM, JOHN LOYER, DAN PANAGGIO
TRAINER: JAY JENSEN

Shareef Abdur-Rahim, Derek Anderson, Maurice Baker, Geno Carlisle, Richie Frahm, Ha Seung Jin, Viktor Khryapa, Darius Miles, Travis Outlaw, Ruben Patterson, Joel Przybilla, Zach Randolph, Theo Ratliff, Damon Stoudamire, Sebastian Telfair, James Thomas, Nick Van Exel

2005–06 (21–61)
COACH: NATE MCMILLAN
ASSISTANT COACHES: BOB BURKE, DEAN DEMOPOULOS, MAURICE LUCAS, MONTY WILLIAMS
TRAINER: JAY JENSEN

Steve Blake, Juan Dixon, Ha Seung Jin, Jarrett Jack, Viktor Khryapa, Voshon Lenard, Darius Miles, Sergei Monia, Travis Outlaw, Ruben Patterson, Joel Przybilla, Zach Randolph, Theo Ratliff, Brian Skinner, Charles Smith, Sebastian Telfair, Martell Webster

2006–07 (32–50)
COACH: NATE MCMILLAN
ASSISTANT COACHES: BILL BAYNO, DEAN DEMOPOULOS, MAURICE LUCAS, MONTY WILLIAMS
TRAINER: JAY JENSEN

LaMarcus Aldridge, Dan Dickau, Juan Dixon, Stephen Graham, Jarrett Jack, Freddy Jones, Raef LaFrentz, Jamaal Magloire, Travis Outlaw, Joel Przybilla, Zach Randolph, Jeremy Richardson, Sergio Rodriguez, Brandon Roy, Luke Schenscher, Ime Udoka, Martell Webster

2007–08 (41–41)
COACH: NATE MCMILLAN
ASSISTANT COACHES: BILL BAYNO, DEAN DEMOPOULOS, MAURICE LUCAS, MONTY WILLIAMS
TRAINER: JAY JENSEN

LaMarcus Aldridge, Steve Blake, Channing Frye, Taurean Green, Jarrett Jack, Freddy Jones, Raef LaFrentz, Josh McRoberts, Travis Outlaw, Joel Przybilla, Sergio Rodriguez, Brandon Roy, Von Wafer, Martell Webster

2008–09 (54–28, PLAYOFFS 2–4)
COACH: NATE MCMILLAN
ASSISTANT COACHES: BILL BAYNO, KALEB CANALES, DEAN DEMOPOULOS, MAURICE LUCAS, JOE PRUNTY, MONTY WILLIAMS
TRAINER: JAY JENSEN

LaMarcus Aldridge, Nicolas Batum, Jerryd Bayless, Steve Blake, Ike Diogu, Rudy Fernandez, Channing Frye, Greg Oden, Travis Outlaw, Joel Przybilla, Shavlik Randolph, Sergio Rodriguez, Brandon Roy, Michael Ruffin, Martell Webster

2009–10 (50–32, PLAYOFFS 2–4)
COACH: NATE MCMILLAN
ASSISTANT COACHES: BILL BAYNO, KALEB CANALES, DEAN DEMOPOULOS, MAURICE LUCAS, JOE PRUNTY, MONTY WILLIAMS
TRAINER: JAY JENSEN

LaMarcus Aldridge, Nicolas Batum, Jerryd Bayless, Steve Blake, Marcus Camby, Dante Cunningham, Travis Diener, Rudy Fernandez, Juwan Howard, Andre Miller, Patrick Mills, Greg Oden, Travis Outlaw, Joel Przybilla, Shavlik Randolph, Brandon Roy, Anthony Tolliver, Martell Webster

(left) Rasheed Wallace
(opposite) Brandon Roy celebrates after making a 30-foot game winning shot in overtime against Houston on November 6, 2008.

BRANDON ROY PROVED HE'S AMONG THE NBA ELITE

When Brandon Roy scored a career-high 52 points seven days before Christmas 2008, he firmly entrenched himself not only as the Blazers' do-everything leader, but also as one of the best players in the NBA—conceivably for years to come.

While Roy hadn't as yet been embraced as one of the league's elite, he clearly was no Piltdown Man. That paleontological hoax was shot down in 1953, proving that you can't judge a man, even an early one, on face value. Even though Roy's point explosion in a 124–119 win over Phoenix at the Rose Garden was as authentic as an individual basketball achievement can get, his teammates, and players and coaches around the league, treated it like the first coming of a franchise savior.

"This might be the top performance I've ever seen," said Blazer point guard Steve Blake. "I'm not sure what else compares. Nothing comes to mind."

Meanwhile, Byron Scott, who coached New Orleans at the time, had this to say when he learned that Roy had scored 52: "As coaches, when we scout Portland, we kind of put him in the same category of Kobe [Bryant], LeBron [James], Dwyane Wade. We treat him the same. He's that good."

Roy made 14 of 27 shots from the field, including 5 of 7 from 3-point range, and 19 of 21 free throws. He added 6 assists, 5 rebounds, and a block. "This is the best game I've played," Roy said. "I've never scored [that many], even in Little League."

MILLER GETS 52 THE OLD-FASHIONED WAY

Andre Miller had a reputation during his 11-year NBA career as a playmaker, certainly not as a shooter. Yet he shocked fans, teammates, and NBA pundits alike on January 30, 2010, at Dallas when he scored an old-fashioned "no big deal" 52 points to lead the Blazers to an upset 114–112 overtime win over the Mavericks.

"That is one dude who does not care—anything it takes to win, that's all he cares about," marveled teammate Martell Webster. "He came in here like nothing happened."

"Yeah," LaMarcus Aldridge said. "He's in here acting like he had 10 points. I'm like, 'Andre, how about some emotion? How about some excitement?' His answer, with a smile: 'We won.'"

Nicolas Batum, when recounting Miller's night, speculated that Miller may have never left his feet: "He never jumped once," Batum said, drawing laughter from Aldridge and Webster.

A night after going 1 for 6 for 2 points in 21 minutes at Houston, Miller was 22 of 31 from the floor and 7 of 8 from the foul line at Dallas, setting Portland's all-time record for field goals made. He finished with a career-high 52 points in 42 minutes, while taking, and making, only one 3-pointer.

What made Miller's performance most astonishing are three factors: (1) His total was 15 points more than he had ever scored before in his life. (2) He hit jumpers, two-handed set shots, driving layups with either hand, put backs, post-ups, and, perhaps the most important one of all, a running right-handed hook shot in the lane that tied the score in regulation with 14.5 seconds left to go. (3) The first shot he took missed everything except the other side of the backboard. Who knew?

Clyde Drexler addresses the media.

2·0

208 209
Entry All

106 EXIT 107

FIVE
15

22

SPALDING

Northwest Ford Stores

Ford
COMPAREFORD.COM

40

ripcity

ACKNOWLEDGMENTS

When you are assigned to research and write a history book covering forty years, you have more people to thank than there are names in your Rolodex. So while recognizing those I left out with a sincere apology, here is my list of 40 special contributors, all of whom, at one time or another, lightened the load.

The first team: Chuck Charnquist, Jim Taylor, Bill Schonely, Bruce Ely, Michael Miller, Bucky Buckwalter, Harry Glickman, Stuart K. Inman, Kerry Eggers, Jason Quick.

The second team: John White, Cheri White Hanson, Collin Romer, Tim Denny, Bill Walton, Ron Culp, Aaron Grossman, Jim Barnett, Dwight Jaynes, Geoff Petrie.

The third team: Bill Evans, Casey Holdahl, David Halberstam, Larry Colton, Terry Porter, Dale Schlueter, Rick Adelman, Brad Weinrich, Nate McMillan, Scott Lynn.

Others: John Canzano, John Bassett, Kenny Wheeler, Joe Freeman, Rich Patterson, Larry Steele, Laura Green, Kris Kolvisto, Larry Mudrick, Terry Durham.

A special "you know best" award goes to my editor, Kevin Toyama of Insight Editions, for his editing suggestions, deletions, and enhancements that helped make the rhythm of the book work more like a fast break than a slow-down, half-court read.

And the biggest hugs of all to my wife, M'Lou, a retired English teacher, who edited, from start to finish, 11 drafts of the book without a single turnover.

COLOPHON

Publisher: **RAOUL GOFF**
Creative Director: **IAIN R. MORRIS**
Executive Editor: **SCOTT GUMMER**
Managing Editor: **KEVIN TOYAMA**
Production Director: **ANNA WAN**

Insight Editions would like to thank Barbara Genetin, Navid Maghami, Martina D'Alessandro, Charles Gerli, Kevin Finley, and Jason Babler.

Trail Blazers Project Editor: **JIM TAYLOR**
Trail Blazers Art Director: **RYAN FLAHERTY**
Trail Blazers Archivist: **CHUCK CHARNQUIST**
Designer: **SCOTT ANTHONY ERWERT**
Photo Editor: **BRUCE ELY**
Copy Editor: **KATHERINE WRIGHT**
Proofreader: **MIKAYLA BUTCHART**

I ATTENDED THE
Portland trail blazers
300th
CONSECUTIVE SELL OUT
~~February 19, 1984~~
March 3, 1984
BLAZERS VS. ~~BOSTON~~ INDIANA